"Go and make disciples of all nations, baptising them in the name of the Father and of the Son and of the Holy Spirit, and teaching them to obey everything I have commanded you. And surely I am with you always, to the very end of the age."

Matthew 28:19–20

"You will receive power when the Holy Spirit comes on you; and you will be my witnesses in Jerusalem, and in all Judea and Samaria, and to the ends of the earth."

Acts 1:8

Defining Moments:
Ordinary Men & Women on Extraordinary Missions
© 2018 by Our Daily Bread Ministries
Published by Discovery House Publishing Singapore Pte. Ltd.
All rights reserved.

Discovery House Publishing™ is affiliated with Our Daily Bread Ministries Asia Ltd.

Requests for permission to quote from this book should be directed to:
Permissions Department
Our Daily Bread Publishing
P.O. Box 3566
Grand Rapids, MI 49501
Or contact us by email at permissionsdept@odb.org.

Image used under license from *Shutterstock.com*
Design by Joshua Tan

Defining Moments

Ordinary Men & Women on Extraordinary Missions

Leslie Koh

Contents

Introduction

Few works can adequately capture the dedication and passion that missionaries over the centuries have displayed in their commitment to bring the gospel to those who have yet to hear of Jesus Christ. It is impossible to tell the stories of the hundreds and thousands of men and women who have given up their lives to make disciples of all people, and it is certainly challenging to do justice to their efforts and sacrifices. So it is with great humility that we attempt to re-tell the stories of eight past missionaries who reached out to people across the Asia-Pacific, using material taken from their autobiographies and biographies, or from the wealth of information documenting their lives and work. At the same time, we look to the future too, with a young missionary sharing his story in his own words.

These nine missionaries are no more and no less special than anyone else who has obeyed Jesus' command to witness for Him. We picked them simply because we wanted you to learn about some of the men and women who have brought the gospel to unreached parts of Asia. You may be familiar with some of these names, while others may be generally less prominent; however, the Lord God knows them all!

Without downplaying their successes, we also take heart in the fact that all these missionaries are, at the end of the day, ordinary men and women. Like every one of us, they had very human fears and anxieties about accepting God's call. Many felt they had no talent or skill that God could possibly use, wondered if they were up to the job, or worried about their families and other commitments. So what made them obey? What gave them the faith to say, "Here I am, Lord. Send me"?

We have thus chosen to focus not so much on the accomplishments and exploits of these missionaries in the field, for there are already many excellent biographies for this purpose, but on the turning points in their lives that transformed them from ordinary men and women into pillars of faith. In doing so, we hope to offer you a glimpse into their hearts and minds as they made the crucial decisions that changed the lives and destinies of themselves and many others. Like them, every one of us can be Christ's witness, for ultimately it is the Holy Spirit who empowers us.

"You will receive power when the Holy Spirit comes on you; and you will be my witnesses in Jerusalem, and in all Judea and Samaria, and to the ends of the earth" (Acts 1:8).

One

A Significant Death
Adoniram Judson

Adoniram Judson (1788–1850) was one of the first missionaries to enter Burma (known as Myanmar today). The American-born evangelist had meant to go to India, but God led him to Burma, where he spent the rest of his life bringing the gospel to a nation who had not heard of Jesus. When he arrived, there were virtually no known Christians in the country. By the time he died, there were 63 churches and 7,000 converts. Today, the church in Myanmar has more than six million Christians. Its growth owes much to Adoniram's tireless efforts in ministering to people, spreading the gospel, and translating the Bible into Burmese.

Someone was dying next door. Groans and gasps filtered through the walls of the little inn as people went in and out of the room, discussing in hushed tones what else could be done for the dying man.

Adoniram Judson was not surprised, because the keeper of the village inn outside New York City had pretty much told him so when he asked for a room that night in 1808. There was only one vacant room, next to a man who was critically ill, the innkeeper had said apologetically, so would he mind sleeping next door?

Adoniram had shaken his head dismissively. Death, he declared, held no terrors for him. After all, he was an atheist and a sceptic. As far as he was concerned, God and the spiritual world did not exist. And even if they did, whatever deity there was surely had no interest in the affairs of men. What did he have to fear?

Such ideas had come from a fellow student at the College of Rhode Island and Providence Plantations—Brown University today. Jacob Eames, an intelligent, witty senior, had welcomed Adoniram into a circle of rich, cultured intellectuals who embraced such philosophies. Over the course of many conversations, Jacob had convinced him that God really didn't care about people. This seemed to be a logical conclusion when reason was applied to the study of philosophy, history, science, politics, economics, and social issues. It was a popular idea; a large majority of students were embracing this approach, shaking off their seemingly outdated, traditional ideas, and upbringing.

Adoniram was so taken in by this philosophy that while still in college, he decided to give up his Christian faith. His parents were devastated. His father was a preacher who had once looked on proudly as his precocious three-year-old, coached by his wife, read him a chapter from the Bible. That three-year-old had grown up into a bright young man who consistently did well in school and graduated top of his class in college, and whose keen intellect and talent for languages boded well for his future. Perhaps, Adoniram Judson Senior had once thought his son might even follow in his footsteps and join the ministry.

On his twentieth birthday, however, the younger Adoniram dropped a bombshell. He had, he told his father, abandoned his childhood faith some time ago. Their sharp exchange of words brought his mother to tears, but the young man refused to listen to her pleas. Forget theology, he said, he was going to New York City to join the theatre.

Attaching himself to a group of itinerant actors, Adoniram toured several American states on horseback, living the adventure-filled life of his dreams. Not long after, he found himself stopping for the night at a village inn just outside the city.

Now, however, disturbing thoughts skimmed across Adoniram's mind as he lay in bed, kept awake by the sounds of agony and despair filtering through the thin walls. *Was the poor man*, he wondered, *ready to face death*? Was he, Adoniram, ready to face death? Where would he go after death? Would it make a difference if he was a Christian? Would he be heading for the hell he had been taught about?

Adoniram tried to quash these thoughts. *What foolishness,* he corrected himself. These things weren't supposed to bother an atheist, were they? What would his compatriots say if they knew?

Turning over in bed, Adoniram tried to ignore the groans. Finally, after some hours, the room next door fell quiet. *Perhaps,* he thought, *the poor man had finally taken a turn for the better. Or . . .* he shuddered to think the worst.

When the sun rose the next morning, Adoniram jumped out of bed. He had barely slept, and couldn't wait to find out what had happened to his neighbour. He wasn't too surprised when the innkeeper told him that the man had died during the night. "Do you know who he was?" Adoniram asked. He was stunned to hear the reply.

"Oh yes. Young man from the college in Providence; name was Eames, Jacob Eames."[1]

Jacob! Jacob, full of life and vigour, who had once laughingly proclaimed grand plans to become a senator and maybe even run for the presidency. Jacob, the man who had taught him that God didn't exist and that there was nothing to fear from death. Jacob, who had spent the last night of his life groaning in agony and pain—and possibly in fear of what awaited him on the other side of death.

Adoniram felt the world drop out from under his feet. "Jacob—dead! Lost! Lost!" he muttered to himself.[2] All the wonderful ideas he had embraced in the last few years suddenly ceased to matter. For all his disbelief in the spiritual world, hell had suddenly become real; it had reached out into that country inn and snatched Jacob, his dearest friend, from the next bed.

Lost! Adoniram could not get the words out of his mind. Lost! Jacob was lost! And then, it struck him: he, Adoniram, was lost.

All of a sudden, the joy and excitement of his travels evaporated, along with his wanderlust and dreams of fame and glory. What would it matter, achieving everything in the world, if hell came and snatched him away one day, just as it had Jacob? How would worldly success save him from the terrors beyond the grave? A cold hand gripped Adoniram's heart as he pondered his future. The ground shifted beneath his feet, and he could feel himself slipping, sliding into the abyss.

At that moment, Adoniram was sure of only one thing: he had to go home and ask his father about God. He had to find out what life, death, and eternity were all about. Adoniram Judson would never forget the death of Jacob Eames.

"What will you have me to do?"

In October 1808, Adoniram enrolled at Andover Theological Seminary, a changed man. No longer an atheist, he knew what his goal in life was: not the honours bestowed by man, but the approval of the divine. "More than all else, I long to please you, Lord," he once prayed. "What will you have me to do?"[3] Adoniram was sure that he was meant to have but one purpose in life: to serve and please his Lord. Only the "how" remained.

The answer arrived in September 1809. One day, he read an account by a former chaplain about the "Star in the East". It detailed the opportunities for spreading the gospel in the wake of British expansion into Asia. As the great trading companies expanded operations across India and East Asia, they were paving the way for missionaries to enter distant territories that had yet to hear the Word of God. The message was clear: roads were opening for the passage of the gospel.

The report struck a chord in Adoniram. Wasn't that exactly what Christ wanted His followers to do? Didn't his Lord command him to "go and make disciples of all nations, baptising them in the name of the Father and of the Son and of the Holy Spirit, and teaching them to obey everything I have commanded you" (Matthew 28:19–20)?

For days after, Adoniram could think of nothing else. The urgency of the report and of Christ's Great Commission filled his mind and dominated his thoughts, along with romantic images of himself roaming Asia, telling people about Jesus' death and resurrection. What really bothered him, however, was the idea that thousands of people were dying every day in hopelessness, borne down by their sin—just as Jacob had.

Unable to focus on his studies, he went round talking to classmates and friends about the urgent need for missions. To his joy, he found some who shared the same burden, and soon they were meeting regularly to pray—for more people to come to a saving knowledge of Christ, and for God to open doors so they could spread such knowledge overseas. These prayer sessions had been sparked by the famous Haystack Meeting, so named because it had been held in the shelter of a haystack. They marked the birth of missions in America. For Adoniram, they would also mark the beginning of his ministry—and a life filled with much adventure, pain, joy, grief, disappointment, and satisfaction.

In 1812, after marrying, he set sail for Calcutta, India. The local colonial authorities, however, did not welcome missionaries, whose preaching might inflame communal tensions and disrupt their profitable trading arrangements. Undeterred, he moved to Burma, where he spent the next 38 years of his life—returning to America only once—preaching the gospel to thousands of people who had never heard of Jesus.

"Don't turn a deaf ear!"

Much has been written about Adoniram's travails in Burma. He was widowed twice and seven of his 13 children died young. When war broke out between Britain and Burma, the English-speaking American was falsely accused of being an enemy spy. Hauled to prison, he spent more than a year and a half in dire conditions, his feet chained in irons. Many of his fellow prisoners died in captivity before he was released in November 1825.

The work of the ministry was also tough. Six long years passed before Adoniram finally saw the first convert baptised in June 1819. "Oh, may it prove to be the beginning of a series of baptisms in the Burman empire which shall continue in uninterrupted success to the end of the age," he wrote in his journal.[4] He never gave up his faith in the power of the gospel, despite knowing how hard it could be to bridge vast cultural and language divides, reaching out to people who were resistant or even hostile to Christianity. It took another three to four years before the number of converts rose to 18.

While in Burma, he wrote letters back home urging more to join him. Don't turn a deaf ear, he told his readers, "to the plaintive cry of millions of immortal beings, who, by their darkness and misery, cry, day and night, 'Come to our rescue, ye bright sons and daughters of America. Come and save us, for we are sinking into hell!'"[5]

He also warned would-be missionaries not to lose sight of the cause to which the Lord himself had called them. "Satan," he wrote, "will sympathise with you in the matter and he will present some chapel of ease in which to officiate in your native tongue, some government situation, some professorship or editorship, some literary or scientific pursuit, some supernumerary translation, or, at least, some system of schools; anything, in a word, that will help you, without much surrender of character, to slip out of real missionary work."[6]

In the meantime, Adoniram persevered in preaching and in translating the Bible into the Burmese language, which he had painstakingly learnt. He was adamant that people needed to hear and read God's Word in their own language. He also compiled a Burmese-English dictionary which became the basis for all subsequent dictionaries and grammar books written in the country.

In 1827, Adoniram made contact with the indigenous Karen tribes, becoming the first missionary to bring God's Word to them. The Karen people in turn would produce the country's first native pastor.

Throughout his 38 years in Burma, Adoniram was driven by a deep desire to make sure that more people would come to know the Lord, and receive the forgiveness of sin and hope of everlasting life. He would never forget the death that had set him on this path. Jacob Eames, the man who had so confidently proclaimed his atheism, died without the hope of salvation. And if Adoniram Judson could help it, no one would die like Jacob again.

Two

Going Native
George Leslie Mackay

George Leslie Mackay (1844–1901) spent most of his life evangelising in the north of Formosa, the island known as Taiwan today. God gave the Canadian missionary such a deep, intense love for the land, its people, and their culture that he adopted much of their ways—so much so that he became known as "the son-in-law of Taiwan". Hailed by many as one of the greatest evangelists of his time, George left a legacy that included thousands of converts, scores of churches, a hospital, a girls' school, and a training centre for church leaders that formed the foundation of the Taiwan Theological College and Seminary.

News of the marriage came as a shock. George Leslie Mackay, the 34-year-old "black-bearded barbarian" missionary, had tied the knot with a Taiwanese aboriginal girl half his age. Tiu Chhang Mia, the adopted granddaughter of Thah-so, George's first woman convert, was a "Pe-po-hoan", or what the ethnic Chinese on the island derogatively called the "barbarians of the plain".[1]

The marriage, which took place on 27 May 1878 in the Tamsui district at the northern tip of the island of Formosa—as Taiwan was known then—was controversial and frowned upon by many of his fellow Canadian pastors and the foreign expatriate community on the island. This was, after all, taking place in an era when many Westerners believed in their superiority. A Caucasian married to an aboriginal girl? "Disgraceful," muttered some.

Even worse, George seemed to have married the girl as a deliberate snub to matchmaking attempts by others. The Women's Foreign Missionary Committee had been trying to send single women teachers to help him, in the hope of hooking him up with a suitable mate for his work. Not only had he rebuffed them, but he had also made clear his opinion of women missionaries from the West. As far as he was concerned, they would not be able to adapt to the tropical climate and the hardships of pioneering missions work, and would never be fully accepted by those they reached out to.

To locals on Formosa, however, the marriage was nothing short of sensational. The "barbarian" had abandoned his own race and become one of them! It was cause for celebration indeed. He was no longer a foreign missionary, he was a son-in-law; he was family.

Some biographers would later suggest that this was exactly what George wanted when he chose to marry Chhang Mia. It was a brilliant, calculated move, they observed, as it won the hearts of the locals and showed that George had genuinely embraced their culture. George himself had once noted, "I am thinking how I can do most for Jesus."[2]

We will never know what George was thinking—or feeling—when he decided to make Chhang Mia his soulmate and missions partner for life. What is certain, however, is that the marriage reflected and cemented a principle that he had espoused since he arrived on the island of Formosa on 29 December 1871: any ministry to evangelise in a foreign land would succeed only if it was truly native.

From day one, George had gone all out to integrate with the people to whom God had sent him. He had learnt to speak Hokkien, the Chinese dialect spoken by most islanders, fluently. This was no mean feat, given that most Westerners had trouble with the multiple "tones" in Chinese that were alien to European languages. He spent more time with the locals than his own people, and grew to prefer their company to that of other Westerners. He developed a genuine fascination for all things Taiwanese, from its culture and traditions to its flora and fauna, and amassed a respectable collection that sits in several museums today. He would later document his discoveries of the island and its people in a book, *From Far Formosa: The Island, Its People, and Missions*, which became an important source of anthropological information to historians and scholars of his day.

But even more importantly, George had fought a constant battle against efforts by his own superiors and church back home to establish Western influences on the mission in north Formosa. He had insisted on training and empowering local preachers to reach out to their own people, rebuffing repeated attempts to appoint Western missionaries to oversee mission efforts and church planting.

"A native ministry for the native church," he would say.[3] It was a principle George had come up with even before he left Canada, and one that he would maintain until his death in 1901.

From Canadian to Chinese

Born in 1844 in Zorra, a town of Oxford County, near Ontario, George decided to become a missionary when he was just 10 years old. That decision came after Scottish missionaries, including William C. Burns—well known for his missionary work in China—visited Zorra and inspired the young George. "His name was cherished in the home, and something of his spirit touched my boyish heart," he said of his boyhood hero. "The command,

'Go ye into all the world, and preach the gospel to every creature' made me a soldier of the cross. To be a missionary became the passion of my life."[4]

This ambition led George to pursue theological training at Knox College in Toronto and Princeton Theological Seminary in the United States, both of which were well known for training missionaries, and to study under another boyhood hero, pioneer missionary to India Alexander Duff. Duff, the first overseas missionary of the Church of Scotland, saw education as a vital key to missions and did much for the development of higher education over his 30-plus years in India. In 1871, the Canada Presbyterian Church commissioned George as its first overseas missionary. Soon after, the 27-year-old was on his way to Formosa.

By that time, George had already acquired a reputation for being somewhat eccentric. Some described him as "an excited young man"; in turn, he criticised the church leadership for their "ice age" thinking.[5]

Arriving in Takao—Kaohsiung today—on 29 December 1871, George discovered that there was no missionary operating in the northern part of the island and thus decided to make Tamsui his base of operations. Located near the northernmost tip of the island, the district sat just north-west of Taipei, where the Tamsui River meets the Taiwan Strait. Following Duff's advice, George immediately went about training locals to teach, preach, evangelise, and lead the chapels that he established, believing that only native preachers could be truly effective at reaching out to their people. He also took pains to avoid applying Western missional methods and approaches wholesale to his task. Anyone who held to a universal approach of sharing the gospel without taking into account the influence of local culture, languages, traditions, and even climate, he maintained, would be making a "grievous mistake". "What would be reasonable and effective in one field would be absurd and useless in another. What would succeed in Europe or America would fail in Asia," he wrote.[6]

In keeping with this belief, George pursued a practice of total cultural assimilation throughout his time on Formosa. He maintained minimal social contact with other Europeans, lived among the common folk, and spoke and preached in their local dialect, which he learnt from local boys who herded cattle.

Even then, George could not completely avoid the racial epithets that came from the locals. He got used to being called a "foreign devil" and "barbarian", to the unfriendly looks, and even to the raw eggs, human waste, and stones that were sometimes hurled at him. In fact, these were nothing compared to the actual persecution that George and his fellow missionaries suffered in their ministry over the years. They were often physically attacked when they entered villages to share the gospel, with George narrowly avoiding serious injury on several occasions. Those opposed to the spread of Christianity hounded local pastors and converts, disrupted church services, and started riots against

Christians. In 1884, when George was forced to evacuate from the island in the midst of the Sino-French war, local Chinese attacked, tortured, killed converts, and destroyed some of the chapels they had built. Unruffled, George demanded compensation when he returned and built new stone churches, prompting his persecutors to complain that "we cannot stop the barbarian missionary".[7]

A single-minded determination to witness for the Lord drove George to persevere through the myriad persecutions and challenges that he faced on Formosa. He won his first convert in his first month on the island. Giam Cheng-hoa, an educated man and his Chinese tutor, accepted Christ and later became Formosa's first ordained native pastor.

George's gospel outreach was accompanied by an unusual ministry: when not preaching to villagers, he was pulling out their teeth. Armed with rudimentary tools and medicines, he would try to alleviate toothaches and tropical diseases.

Training local pastors, however, remained his highest priority. George began an itinerant ministry that combined gospel outreach and a moving "theological school" for young men who were ready to dedicate their lives to the Lord. For months at a time, George travelled with them around northern Formosa to bring the good news to ethnic Chinese villagers as well as aboriginal tribes. During these trips, he gave his recruits both theological and secular training, teaching them about the Bible, history, and science. In turn, they taught him about Chinese culture and improved his grasp of Hokkien. Many of these young men went on to start and pastor churches of their own.

That itinerant ministry evolved into a more permanent one in 1882, when the finishing touches were made to Oxford College. Funded by supporters in George's hometown—thanks to successful fund-raising efforts by his wife Chhang Mia—it was named after Oxford County and allowed George to extend his educational efforts to more local students. While it included Western-style courses on secular subjects, the curriculum remained big on practical theological training and evangelism. It included regular mission trips that took students to Formosa's unreached villages, where they had to preach and learn to deal with opposition to the Christian faith—experience and skills that these students would need when they became pastors of their own churches one day.

George's unrelenting focus on evangelism and training paid off. In his first few years, his itinerant ministry saw the creation of no less than seven chapels in Formosa's interior, with more than 20 local men teaching and preaching every week. The number of churches would grow to 16 by 1888 and more than 60 by the time of his death.

Indeed, many of the Canadian's often-controversial actions and eccentric evangelistic methods would ultimately prove successful during his 30 years on Formosa. Despite the initial storm that his marriage to Chhang Mia caused, she became a formidable partner in his ministry. During a trip to Canada in 1881, it was

Chhang Mia who raised some $6,000 for the construction of Oxford College. And when the college was expanded to include a girls' boarding school, she became its matron and, together with other older women, taught and mentored the girls. As George had predicted, she proved to be more effective than any woman sent from Canada could have been.

"She knew just how to deal with her own people," said Annie Jamieson, the wife of one of George's assistants. "She works away [at] training girls, helping women, attending to the wants of students, caring for and thinking of everyone but herself. She is known and loved by converts throughout the whole field."[8]

George and Chhang Mia had three children—a son and two daughters. The two girls married local preachers.

A Lasting Legacy

By the time of George Mackay's death from cancer in 1901, there was no longer any doubt about the effectiveness of his long-held principle of raising native workers for a native ministry. Of course, George himself had mellowed over the years, and acknowledging the value of the Presbyterian-led ministry in the southern half of Formosa, he said, "Although our methods of work differ very materially, we are 'one in hope and doctrine, one in charity' . . . God has no fixed method by which his servants must work, and each according to his ability and his circumstances must serve our common Master."[9]

In the northern half of the island, George left a legacy that has endured to this day. The schools that he founded paved the way for modern education in Taiwan, and Oxford College (now Aletheia University) became recognised as a pioneer institution of higher learning. A medical clinic that he built became Mackay Hospital, and was later relocated to downtown Taipei as Mackay Memorial Hospital.

More importantly, the numerous chapels that George founded eventually formed the bedrock of the Presbyterian Church in northern Taiwan. By giving local preachers more autonomy and freedom than most Western missionaries of his day had done, he helped them achieve a self-sufficiency that played an important role in powering the growth of churches on the island. His influence even extended back home, where his exploits inspired young people to become missionaries, just as he himself had once been inspired by Alexander Duff.

But what George will be most remembered for is the way he identified himself with the people of Formosa. His complete devotion and genuine interest in the people he cared for, and his determination to overcome cultural, language, and racial barriers in his ministry, reflected God's abiding love for His people and won many hearts for the Lord. As Mackay scholar Professor James Rohrer put it, George's ministry showed how cultural differences can be bridged by bonds built through mutual affection and respect. "George Leslie Mackay allowed himself to truly encounter and to be transformed by the people he sought to serve," he wrote. "This desire to become one with the people, to identify with them as wholly as he possibly could, deeply touched many of those whom he encountered."[10]

For George himself, all this was nothing more than a deep, intense love for Formosa and its people. The island, he wrote, "is dear to my heart". He loved its mountains, its valleys, its waters, and its people. "To serve them in the gospel," he declared, "I would gladly, a thousand times over, give up my life."[11]

This love was expressed in a poem, "My Final Resting Place":[12]

How dear is Formosa to my heart!
On that island the best of my years have been spent.
How dear is Formosa to my heart!
A lifetime of joy is centred here.
I love to look up to its lofty peaks, down into its yawning
chasms, and away out on its surging seas.
How willing I am to gaze upon these forever!
My heart's ties to Taiwan cannot be severed!
To that island I devote my life.
My heart's ties to Taiwan cannot be severed! There I find my joy.
I should like to find a final resting place within sound of
its surf and under the shade of its waving bamboo.

Three

The Call of the Wild
James Matthew Hoover

James Matthew Hoover (1872–1935) was sent by the Methodist Church in America to Sarawak—now part of East Malaysia—to shepherd some of the first Chinese Christian settlers on Borneo. Apart from preaching to them and teaching them God's Word, the lay preacher spent much of his 30-plus years with the villagers improving their standard of living through education and social, economic, and technological development. He introduced many things to them, from the first girls' school and rice mill to the first bicycle and motor boat. Unlike some other missionaries, James did not experience a dramatic calling; instead, God spoke to him softly and gently, leading James into a life of ministry that would eventually result in more than 40 churches, more than 40 schools, and a legacy of Christian faith and missions in Sarawak.

The paper lay on the reading table in the sitting room day after day, as if demanding to be read repeatedly. Normally, any document that made its way into the Hoover home in Chambersburg, Pennsylvania, would have been put away at the end of the day by Ma Hoover. For some reason, however, she had decided to leave the church paper on the table that fateful week in early 1899.

Titled "A Call to Our Young Men", it was written by a Methodist bishop who had helped establish one of India's largest churches and was now also overseeing missionary efforts in Malaya (Malaysia today). The paper contained a simple plea: 12 young men were needed to help spread the gospel in India. It was not meant to be an attractive proposal—the paper stated clearly that the men should not expect much pay; were to raise their own support while serving in the field; were expected to serve five years; and were to carry out whatever task was needed wherever they were sent to. As for any thought of marriage—well, that was to be postponed until they had served their time.

It didn't make for terribly entertaining reading, yet it seemed to call out to James, the elder of the two sons of John Hoover, a shoemaker, and his wife Emily. Day after day, the 26-year-old teacher came back from work at noon, expecting to see the table cleared. But the paper was always there, its title—and call for 12 willing men—right on top. "It got on my nerves," he would say of it later.[1]

The paper irritated him because it seemed to be written just for him. Wasn't it what he had always dreamt of doing? Wasn't it what he believed God had called him to do?

A little over 10 years ago, at the age of 15, James had got down on his knees in the local church, dedicated his life to God, and promised to serve in whatever capacity God directed him to. Since then, he had tried to make good on his word. He had joined the Young Men's Christian Association (YMCA), where he helped organise wholesome activities for young people to keep them from going morally astray. He had begun serving as a lay preacher in his own church and others in the area, and had also started regular services for prisoners in the county jail. And he had begun teaching in an elementary school that had both African-American and white students—an unusual mix for that time.

Now it appeared that God had been preparing James for overseas missions all along. Over the years, the young man had, without realising it, been receiving real-world training not only in preaching and teaching the Bible, but also in organising activities and dealing with foreign traditions and cultures. Yet this wasn't a dramatic call to missions. No voices echoed in James' head, no verses leapt out from the Bible, no strangers appeared to utter prophecies—there was just a growing conviction that he had to obey Jesus' commandment to "go and make disciples of all nations"—the familiar, unforgettable instruction in Matthew 28:19.

But James, taking his usual methodical, deliberate approach to life, did not rush to sign up. Instead, he began to pray about the matter and went round seeking counsel. The first person he asked was his preacher at school. The man immediately replied, "We would hate to lose you—but why not?"[2]

James wasn't sure about taking this advice wholeheartedly. After all, he figured, which preacher would not urge someone to go into missions? So he sought out the person in charge of the Sunday School programme, believing that he might provide a layman's view. To his surprise, the old man nodded and said, "Young man, when I was your age, I had a call to preach the gospel, but I did not heed it. My life has been a failure. My advice is, 'Go'."[3]

With these words ringing in his ears, James went to a third person, a fellow teacher. The teacher looked straight at him and said, "My boy, when I was a young man, I was asked to go as a missionary to the Indians in the West, but I refused. My life has been an uphill fight."

Looking wistfully into the distance, he added, "I believe that call was my opportunity in life, but I missed it. Don't miss yours."[4]

James had heard enough. If he had been asking God for a clear sign, this was it. Three different men had given him exactly the same answer. He knew what his reply to God should be. This was no impulsive, emotional decision—he had given due diligence, as it were, having spent time talking to God about it, thinking about it, and talking to wise men about it. James was certain that God was calling him to overseas missions. Now he just had to respond.

On 13 March 1899, he carefully wrote to the Board of Foreign Missions a letter that would chart the course for the rest of his life. "I have decided to answer the call," he began, before going on to note that while he did not have much in the way of education, he could offer his experience as a preacher, teacher, and organiser. Knowing that the job would be physically as well as spiritually demanding, he added, "My health is good . . . my power of endurance is all right. Last summer when school closed I took a tramp of 500 miles for recreation and made the distance in about 18 tramping days. One day I made 44 miles."[5]

A few months of waiting followed, during which James did not hear from the board. Then, in June, the reply came, asking him to meet the writer of the paper, Bishop J. M. Thoburn, and other members of the board in New York City for a chat. "You'll do," they told him soon after. "When can you start?" James' reply was just as quick and straight to the point: "Any time."[6]

It was then that the board explained, however, that there was a greater urgency for teachers in Penang, Malaya, than for missionaries in India.

Penang? Malaya? James wasn't even sure where that was! To the small-town American, Asia seemed a world away. Most of his friends had probably never even heard of Malaya. But if this was what God wanted—well, James had vowed to be obedient. Hadn't the Holy Spirit empowered all believers to be Jesus' witnesses to the ends of the earth? As far as James was concerned, there was no doubt that the Holy Spirit would be with him, even to the eastern end of the world. What a blessed privilege, to be God's trusted messenger in fulfilling Acts 1:8!

Explaining his decision to his family and friends, however, turned out to be a lot harder. Many had praised his commitment to God's work in the local church, in school, and at the YMCA. But they didn't seem to favour the idea of going beyond their "Jerusalem" to spread the gospel. "You really should think twice, James," some of them said, comparing the bright prospects he had in America with what he was likely to face in the Far East. Others were encouraging, but expressed great sadness at the prospect of never seeing him again. Many missionaries, they knew, had not returned, succumbing to tropical diseases or the travails of witnessing in faraway lands; at the time, it was not uncommon for a missionary to die within two or three years of arriving at a new posting.

The hardest goodbye to say was to his mother, who had been the bedrock of James' life and who had inspired him in his faith. James was scheduled to leave within a month, and as the days passed, each family dinner got more and more emotional. At one of the last meals, James' mother had to force her food down, stopping every few mouthfuls to weep.

On 29 July 1899, James left New York and sailed for Penang.

From Penang to Sibu

Throughout his life as a missionary, James would find his journey marked by small, undramatic steps of faith, rather than the spectacular, impassioned leaps experienced by some of the more "famous" missionaries. The first step he took after arriving in Penang that September was simply to carry out his appointed task as a teacher at the Penang Boys' School. It was a meaningful job, coaching and mentoring young students to walk in the way of the Lord while also equipping them with the knowledge and skills to succeed in their future lives. James fully expected to be doing this for the rest of his life.

A trip to Singapore at the tip of the Malayan peninsula to attend a Methodist conference, however, changed his mind. One of the speakers, Bishop Frank J. Warne, shared an intriguing account of how he had, in Hong Kong, met a group of Chinese emigrants travelling to Sarawak on the island of Borneo. Sarawak's European ruler, the "White Rajah" Charles Johnson Brooke, was seeking to start a new colony, and through some local leaders had convinced several hundred Chinese farmers from China's Foochow province (Fujian today) to move there. Interestingly, many of these immigrants were Christians, having been converted by earlier missionaries, and were members of the Methodist Episcopal Church. Many of them saw this as an opportunity to escape ongoing civil war in China and drought in their hometown.

The Methodist church, meanwhile, saw this as an opportunity to take the gospel deeper into the region.

Bishop Warne went on to highlight the most urgent need: the tiny Chinese colony, he noted, would have no pastor or teacher in Sarawak to guide them on their journey of faith and ensure that they did not fall back into their traditional faiths and practices. "I beseech you in the name of God," he pleaded, "that you select one of your number to be appointed as missionary to the Chinese in Sarawak—and may God help him, for he will have a hard and perhaps dangerous task in that jungle country."[7]

On hearing this, James felt the first stirrings of adventure. Sarawak? Wasn't that the place supposedly inhabited by fearsome head-hunting Dayak tribes who were continually feuding? It sounded terribly frightening—yet exciting. James wondered if he would ever be chosen for this difficult assignment, though he knew he had little to recommend himself. He was still new to Asia's culture, possessed a less-than-rudimentary knowledge of Chinese and Malay, and was not even an ordained preacher. He was right: eventually, an older, more experienced and qualified man was appointed to the job.

James, however, continued to hold on to the hope that someday, he too would be given the opportunity. Patiently and obediently, he went back to Penang, where he continued to attend diligently to the boys' educational, social, and spiritual needs. Whenever he had some free time, however, he would read what little he could find on this mysterious place called Sarawak. The descriptions of its verdant jungles and the Dayak pirates made for fascinating reading, as did the account of how a British national came to rule the area as the "White Rajah".

A busy year passed, and James returned to Singapore for the annual conference. There, Dr B. F. West, the man sent to Sarawak, reported on his work and, noting how physically challenging the task was, asked for a younger replacement. "Borneo," he declared, "needs a man who can look forward to a long lifetime of service."[8]

James' heart skipped a beat. Would he have another shot at this call? Or, would he be returning to Penang once again? The 29-year-old needn't have worried. His name was raised and quickly approved, and by the end of the conference, it had been decided that the next missionary to Rejang River, Sarawak, would be James Matthew Hoover. Yet another small, quiet step had been taken on the missionary's long journey from Pennsylvania, America, to Sarawak, Malaya.

Preparations were quickly made, and it wasn't long before James was on another ship, heading even farther east. Unlike the 1899 trip from America, this one in February 1903 was far shorter, and soon the ship was approaching Kuching, the capital of Sarawak. James looked up into the sky and saw the first rays of sun breaking through the mist enshrouding the town. "Through that circle of heavenly beauty," he would recall later, "we saw the mouth of the river for which we were headed. I was going to my new task with

God's promise flaming from the sky." It was at that point, he said, that he finally felt that "I have been God's man for that part of His world plan".[9]

Sibu's Missionary Pioneer

At Rejang River, James would face an uphill challenge pastoring the fledgling community that had taken hold in a small jungle clearing near the market town of Sibu. With little infrastructure and facilities, the settlers faced great hardships as they tried to grow enough rice to feed themselves while fending off myriad tropical diseases. Tensions were high between the Chinese farmers and the Dayak natives, who resented the encroachment on their land.

James, meanwhile, was still struggling to communicate with his flock. He had managed to learn some Malay and pick up a few Chinese words in the Hokkien dialect while in Penang, but now he had to learn the Foochow dialect. He also had to deal with homesickness and loneliness, although these were greatly reduced when he married Mary Young in 1904.

Still, he plunged wholeheartedly into his task, teaching the Bible to the settlers, encouraging families to persevere in their faith, and training younger men to serve as lay preachers. Driven by the conviction that missionary work encompassed more than just spiritual teaching, James and Mary also spent much of their time seeing to the settlers' practical needs. They knew that the work of supporting the people in their journey of faith could not be divorced from that of improving their lives socially and economically. They helped the villagers establish schools for boys and girls, build houses and roads, and find ways to increase the yield of their crops.

In fact, over his 30-plus years of ministry along the Rejang River, James would establish a reputation for being a pioneer as well as pastor. He introduced many firsts in the fields of transport, agriculture, education, and communication. The long list included the first bicycle and first motorised launch to help farmers transport their produce; the first rubber seedlings and motorised rice huller; the first girls' school and first agriculture school; and the first ice-making machine, motorised saw, power generator, and wireless telegraph machine. He once said, "Next to the churches and schools I have built, and next to the lives I have helped God to make over, I am proudest of my boats."[10]

James also acted as a local judge of sorts for the community, a mediator between the Chinese and Dayaks—who came to respect him—and a go-between for the Foochow Chinese and the British administrators. In 1904, the latter appointed him the "Protector of the Foochows", a post that gave him useful access to the authorities when he needed more land for the settlers, for example. But the biggest honour was the title of "Hoo Sing Sang" (Teacher Hoo) among the Chinese and "Tuan Hoover" (Sir Hoover) among the local Malays. They demonstrated how much respect and affection

James had earned as he went about God's business of shepherding His flock.

By the time James died of malaria in 1935, he and his wife had established 41 churches and 40 schools, and more than a thousand children had been baptised and educated. The tiny village of 500 that he had pastored was now a modern community of thousands, boasting schools, self-supporting churches, and tens of thousands of acres of cultivated land, thanks in part to James' determination to aid the Foochow Chinese in their social and economic development.

Today, there are more than 120 Methodist churches in Sarawak and Sabah, with more than 60,000 worshippers. They mark a legacy of plodding determination, quiet perseverance, and faithful obedience to Jesus' commandment to be His witness to the ends of the earth. From a small town in Pennsylvania to a tiny jungle clearing in Sarawak, James Hoover had taken small steps in faith, letting the growing conviction of God's calling take root in his heart, and responding with everything he had. Then, whenever the going got tough, he had stayed the course, never deviating from the work he believed God had sent him to do.

Four

Into the Madhouse
John Sung

One of China's greatest evangelists, John Sung (1901–1944) has been called the "Wesley of China". He played a key role in the revival movement of the 1920s and 1930s, not just in China, where he was born, but also in Taiwan and throughout Southeast Asia. His fiery, dramatic sermons and rigorous teaching are said to have brought tens of thousands of people to Christ, and Sung is widely credited for the growth of Christianity in China. As a young man, Sung nearly lost his faith; God, however, reached out to him and showed him personally what it meant to be saved by Christ's death and resurrection, and gave him the passion to reach out to others for Jesus.

He was a brilliant student. He had completed his PhD in chemistry in record time, had been appointed associate professor and had been offered several scholarships, and had the promise of a bright, star-filled future before him. But now, John Sung found himself locked up in an asylum for the insane. The authorities at the Union Theological Seminary in New York City believed that he had gone out of his mind.

Fellow students complained that John had been going round the dormitories evangelising—this, in a seminary! Worse still, he had even gone to his lecturers warning them of eternal punishment if they did not repent of their sins. They were not amused.

John's erratic behaviour was a drastic departure from his usual self. Up till then, he had been a thoughtful, reflective young man who had been willing to question some of the tenets of Christianity, as any decent academic should; now, he appeared to have turned into a Bible-thumping preacher. For the past few days, he had been overly emotional, weeping as he told others about how he had been baptised by the Holy Spirit and how his eyes had been opened to the reality of the gospel.

What had gone wrong? Clearly, concluded the president of the seminary, John had studied so hard that something had snapped. The best thing for the poor man, it would seem, was some rest in the sanatorium, which would hopefully give him time to come to his senses.

John reluctantly agreed to be committed to the psychopathic ward of a hospital, although he knew what was really happening. As far as he was concerned, he had just seen the truth. While he had been born into a Christian family and raised by a father who had dedicated his life to preaching the Word, John had not understood the gospel as clearly as he did now. John—mad? Nothing could be further from the truth.

From "Little Pastor" to Sceptic

John was born Zhu En ("God's Grace") in a village in Hinghwa, Fukien Province (Fujian today), China, to a pastor of a local Methodist church. From young, his intelligence set him apart—as did his fiery temper and strong-headed personality. At nine, he accepted Jesus as his Lord and Saviour after a spiritual revival at the local church. It sparked a love for the Bible, prayer, and preaching. Accompanying his father on preaching trips around provincial villages, John became his father's pastoral assistant, and soon, was even standing in at the pulpit whenever his father was too busy or ill. He became known as the "Little Pastor".

Seeing his potential, American missionaries helped John get a scholarship to study at Ohio Wesleyan University in the US. The plan was for the young man to study with an ultimate aim to join the ministry; on arriving, however, John decided to study chemistry. Within three years—instead of the usual four—he got his Bachelor's degree with top honours, which drew the offer of scholarships from several universities, including Harvard. John accepted one from Ohio State University to do a Master's degree, and then went on to complete a PhD, again in record time.

Taking a break for the first time in years, John now found himself in a dilemma. His parents had wanted him to study for the ministry, and this was something he himself had vowed to do when he first dedicated his life to the Lord. But now, with so many opportunities beckoning, it seemed to be a poor option. Ohio State had appointed him an assistant professor in chemistry, Peking University was offering him a post, and there was an offer of a research fellowship in Germany. Besides, the influence of liberal theology, which was popular in academic circles, was starting to give him second thoughts about his faith. Was Jesus truly Lord and Saviour? Or, was he merely a good moral example? John was beginning to wonder.

One evening, while mulling over the options, John seemed to hear God's voice saying, "What good is it for someone to gain the whole world, yet forfeit their soul?" (Mark 8:36). He shook off the feeling. The next day, however, the words came to mind again during a conversation with a liberal professor who said he looked more like a preacher than a scientist.[1] When John told the man that he had originally come to the US to study theology, the professor suggested the Union Theological Seminary in New York City. There, he was told, he could study religion while still holding a liberal stance, satisfy his father's wishes, and keep open the possibility of returning to a scientific career.

It sounded like a great idea. With John's grades and reputation, a full scholarship would come easily, and it didn't take long for the young man to decide. In 1926, John enrolled at Union Theological Seminary, believing he could combine his parents' wishes for him to read theology and his own interests in philosophy and history.

He couldn't have been more mistaken. While there were some among Union who held to the tenets of the Christian faith, many of its lecturers were most liberal in their outlook, and saw Jesus as little more than a historic personality.[2] As far as they were concerned, God was dead and the Bible's claims about Jesus' resurrection were a pack of lies—and any student who thought otherwise was to be derided and laughed at. Influenced by his teachers and classmates, John too began to doubt his own understanding of God. Encouraged by the prevalent culture of liberalism, he began to explore Buddhism and Taoism, religions which most of his countrymen adhered to. Sometimes, he could even be heard chanting Buddhist scriptures in his room.

At the same time, John could not shake off the sense of emptiness that seemed to be steadily consuming his soul. Listening to lectures and meeting academic deadlines didn't seem to help; John's life, it appeared, had little direction, and he was bothered by his own confusion about Christianity. His sombre mood was noted by his teachers, who wondered if the years of intense study had finally begun to push him over the edge. "My soul wandered in a wilderness," he would write of this period later. "I could neither sleep nor eat. My faith was like a leaking, storm-driven ship without captain or compass. My heart was filled with the deepest unhappiness."[3]

Floundering in his faith and desperate for direction, John visited an evangelistic meeting at a New York City church one evening. There, a young girl gave her personal testimony and spoke about Christ's death on the cross. John's classmates looked at each other and smirked in derision, but John hung on to every word. Somehow, he could feel God's presence. He went back again the next night, and the next. Despite what he had been taught at Union, the messages about God's power to redeem struck a chord deep in his heart. Disturbed, he began to skip classes and read the Bible as well as Christian biographies, hoping to discover what it was about the faith that was bothering him so much.

On 10 February 1927, God gave John Sung the answer.

Born Again

That night, as he was praying and reading the Bible, something strange happened. First, a stifling sensation of weight fell on his heart as the magnitude of his sins began to strike him. All the things he had done wrong in his life flashed before his eyes, and it seemed that nothing could remove his guilt. Desperate, John flipped to Luke 23, where he knew he would find the gospel writer's account of the crucifixion. As he read the story, it seemed to come alive in his mind. It was as if he, John, was standing at the foot of the cross, looking up at the dying Jesus and hoping he could be spared punishment for his own sins. Tears rolled down his cheeks as he realised his predicament. Then, as John continued to plead with God for forgiveness, he seemed to hear a gentle voice. "Son," it said, "your sins are forgiven."[4]

All of a sudden, the burden that had been weighing down on him the entire night lifted. There was an overwhelming sensation of warmth and cleansing. At once, John knew exactly what it was— the Holy Spirit, showing him that he was truly forgiven and truly saved. Forgiven! The word sat on his lips like honey, as John savoured its significance. He was lost, but now he was found. He had sinned, but now he was forgiven. He was dead, but now he was born again.

"Hallelujah!" John praised God again and again as he leapt to his feet. The tears could not stop streaming down his cheeks; he had not felt joy like this before—overwhelming joy that flowed through his very being. His next instinct was to rush out of his room and race down the corridor of the dormitory, shouting and praising God. How could he keep it to himself? How could he let his dear friends continue living in their disbelief and darkness? How could he not share with them this amazing discovery? As soon as he could, he began to go round to his teachers and classmates, telling them about what God had done for him and urging them to come to Christ.

With those who were ready to listen, he was gentle and persuasive; with others, he was forceful, even critical. He saved the harshest words for lecturers who had dismissed the Bible's teachings. "You made me lose my faith!" he charged.[5]

Those words didn't go down well. Perturbed by John's sudden change from constant gloom to unrestrained joy, the seminary's authorities reckoned that he had gone mad, and threw him into the insane asylum. They would later report that he had suffered a psychological breakdown and was experiencing hallucinations and visions. Archival records from the seminary appear to differ greatly from the accounts of John and his friends on his behaviour before, during, and after his confinement, dividing opinions on what really happened during the 193 days that John spent in the asylum.[6]

As far as John himself was concerned, however, those six months were a divine arrangement. Locked up in a cell with only his Bible and a pen, John had 193 long days and nights to rest and ruminate on what had happened in the past week and months. Had he really gone mad? Was the incident of February 10 a figment of his imagination? What was he to believe—Union's liberal approach to theology, or the Bible's account of the death and resurrection of Jesus Christ?

There was only one way to find out: read the Bible. So John did— from Genesis to Revelation, cover to cover. Not once, not twice, not even three times—John read the Scriptures 40 times, scouring each book and chapter as he sought to understand his own spiritual awakening. Putting all of his sharp intellect and power of concentration into the task, he devoured the Bible's words, recalled what his father had taught him, and tested them against the reasoning and logic that he had developed as a scientist.

Those 193 days and 40 readings of the Bible marked a crucial point in John's life. Coming right after his spiritual awakening, they built the foundation of his knowledge and understanding of God's Word, empowering him to share the gospel and teach its truths authoritatively. Later, John would call the mental hospital—and not Union—his real theological college.

"Graduation" and Ministry

John was released from the asylum in August 1927, after an American pastor and the Chinese consulate stepped in to negotiate with the seminary; it was agreed that John would be released, on condition that he return to China. Three months later, he was aboard the ship taking him home. As the shores of China loomed in the distance, John weighed his options. With a PhD in chemistry, he could easily get a post as a professor in a university back home. Or, he could dedicate his life to God's work, as he had vowed so long ago.

With little hesitation, John dug into his trunk and pulled out all the academic diplomas and awards he had earned over the eight years in America. Before he boarded the ship, he had already burnt all his theological textbooks, calling them "books of demons".[7] He extracted his doctoral diploma, which he knew his father would be so proud to see, and put it aside. Then he took the rest of the documents up to the ship's deck and hurled them into the sea. As they fluttered into the water, John nodded with satisfaction. He had just made a commitment to the gospel. No more career, no more fame and glory for him; from now on, every moment of his life would be spent winning souls for God. When he stepped off the boat, he would not be Dr John Sung the chemist, but John the evangelist.

Over the next 15 years or so, John would fulfil this commitment with all his heart and soul. He began preaching in his hometown, Hinghwa, and then joined the Bethel Worldwide Evangelistic Band, a group who took God's Word to China's north-eastern, northern, and southern provinces. By some estimates, the band reached out to more than 400,000 people in its first year. After a few years, John decided to leave the group and become a fully-independent itinerant evangelist. He continued to criss-cross China, preaching and teaching in small rural churches.

Around 1935, he began to take his ministry even further afield, visiting Singapore, Malaysia, the Philippines, Thailand, Vietnam, Myanmar, Indonesia, and Taiwan. In all, he would make five journeys to Southeast Asia. Many churches in these countries attribute spiritual revivals to his dramatic sermons and hard-hitting messages, which dealt with the issue of sin in no uncertain terms. As far as John was concerned, praying "Lord, forgive me for I am a sinner" was not enough. He challenged his listeners to repent of specific sins and mend their ways, and his sermons left many people weeping in shame and confessing their wrongdoings publicly. At some churches, he even pinpointed church leaders and pastors, and often offended them by highlighting their sins.

John was also known for his dramatic flair and sense of theatre. Apart from telling his own parables and sharing real-life stories to illustrate his points, he also acted out the parts of biblical characters. Once, he even brought a small coffin onto the stage and jumped into it, to underline how wealth could not save a man from death. He rarely spoke without breaking into song or prayer.

Throughout his ministry, John would depend on two practices that fuelled his passion for God's work: constant prayer and reading the Bible. When he wasn't preaching, he would spend hours conversing with the Lord and reading His Word. Faith, he once said, was "watching God work while on your knees".[8] He challenged followers to dig deeper into the Word of God, organising numerous Bible conferences and teaching from the Bible, book by book.

Burning the candle at both ends, however, didn't do John's health much good. Weakened by intestinal tuberculosis and a punishing preaching schedule, John died on 18 August 1944. He was just 42 years old.

By that time, he had acquired the honour of being known as "China's John the Baptist"; others called him the "Chinese John Wesley".[9] Many people credit his tireless ministry for bringing God's spiritual awakening to Asia. By some estimates, more than 100,000 Chinese had come to know the Lord through his ministry, and many thousands more had re-dedicated their lives to Him after listening to John's sermons and teaching. Today, churches across Southeast Asia still recall his visits fondly, noting how his preaching had sparked revivals in their communities and brought thousands to a saving knowledge of Jesus Christ.

"Dr John Sung was probably the greatest preacher of this century," wrote his friend, veteran missionary William E. Schubert, in his book, *I Remember John Sung*. "I have heard almost all the great preachers from 1910 until now . . . yet John Sung surpassed them all in pulpit power, attested by amazing and enduring results."[10]

Clearly, the "madman" who spent six months in an asylum knew exactly what he was talking about.

Five

The "Failed" Missionary
Gladys May Aylward

Nothing could stop British missionary Gladys May Aylward (1902–1970) from going to China to share the gospel. Rejected by a missions agency and with virtually no funds, she worked to buy her own train ticket and made her way through a war zone to China, where she spent nearly 20 years reaching out to traders and villagers. When another war hit her new hometown, Gladys led some 100 orphans across the mountains to safety. Throughout her time in China, God opened doors—often in dramatic ways—and protected her so that she could keep bringing His good news to the people of China.

The director's voice was kindly and gentle, but his words were no less than devastating.

Gladys had not done well in theology or Chinese. "Not good at all," the man repeated softly. "There seems to be little point in your continuing with your studies here. We accepted you to be trained in good faith, on trial. If you went on, it would be a waste of everyone's time and money . . ."[1]

He trailed off; there was little need to continue. He hadn't used the actual word, but there it was: Gladys had failed the exams to qualify to be a missionary to China.

Failed! Perhaps she shouldn't have been too surprised. After all, she had never been a good student. She had rarely passed an exam, left school at age 14, been working as a maid since, and seemed not to have a head for facts or figures. Worse—and this cut especially deeply—she was told that she was a little too old.

"If you stayed at the China Inland Mission Centre for another three years and then we sent you out," the director explained sympathetically, "you would be about 30 by the time you arrived. Our experience tells us that after the age of 30, unless pupils are quite exceptional, they find it extremely difficult to learn the Chinese language."[2]

That was something the 28-year-old had not expected to hear when she enrolled in the China Inland Mission—OMF International today—to become a missionary to China. She was aware that her poor school grades and lack of useful skills or experience put her at a great disadvantage, but she was hoping that her sincere faith in God and enthusiasm to witness for Him would impress her interviewers. They were impressed; she was given a chance to take one term and prove that she could handle regular study.

So, for three months, Gladys sat through classes on the Bible and missions history that she struggled to grasp, and Chinese language lessons that were even more difficult. The examinations too were a struggle, but she believed God would help her pass. She didn't.

The director's words echoed in her ears and sliced through her very soul. She had to hold back the tears welling up in her eyes. It didn't make sense, she said to herself. She had wanted so much to go to China and tell others about God's everlasting love. Wasn't that what God wanted? Hadn't He confirmed it by giving her a strong conviction about going to China? Had God made a mistake?

"Me, go to China?"

Few would have seen the missionary in Gladys May Aylward when she was young. Born into a working-class family in Edmonton in north London—father a postman and mother a postal worker— she was very short, just five feet tall, and slender.

"Glad", as her friends called her, was high-spirited and seemed keener on acting than preaching. She did not do well at school, though teachers noted her determination in trying to solve problems. After dropping out, she worked as a housemaid, store worker, and nanny. In the evenings, she attended drama classes in the hope of entering theatre.

Brought up as a Christian in the Anglican tradition, Gladys did not give religion much thought. But one day, on her way to a dance in London, she was somehow separated from her friends and found herself caught up in a large crowd heading towards a church. Unable to squeeze her way out, she sat through the meeting and heard a sermon about the importance of missions. It sparked something in her heart, making her wonder whether God would ever call her to share the gospel overseas. When her friends heard about it, they dismissed the idea. "Don't be silly, Glad," they said. "Come with us to the pictures, or to a dance, or to the theatre, or let's go and meet up with those nice chaps we met in the park."[3]

But God had lit the flame in Gladys' heart, and now He began to fan the fire. At a subsequent church meeting, she accepted Jesus Christ as her Saviour and committed her life to Him. She joined the Young Life Campaign, a movement for young people that focused on evangelism, and in one of its magazines read an article about the millions of people in China who had not heard the gospel. The article, she would recall later, made a "terrific impression" on her. "To realise that millions of Chinese had never heard of Jesus Christ was to me a staggering thought, and I felt we ought to do something about it," she said.[4]

In her mind, that "something" had to be done by someone clever or talented. So she approached friends, former employers, and her younger brother Laurence, who was in the army. All of them declined. Laurence was even more direct. "Not me!" he retorted. "That's an old maid's job. Why don't you go yourself?"

At first, his remark angered Gladys. "Old maid's job, indeed!" she thought.[5] Such a job surely required someone intelligent, capable, experienced, and driven, didn't it? How could she fit the bill?

Her brother's words, however, took root in her heart, and for days after their conversation, they kept popping up in her thought. "Why not me?" she began to ask herself. "Why should I push other people off to China? Why don't I go myself?"[6] That thought soon became a conviction, then an outright plan: yes, Gladys would become a missionary herself, and she would go to China.

Her father was sceptical; Gladys could neither nurse nor teach, he pointed out. But she was not to be dissuaded. She even went to London's famous Speakers' Corner to practise preaching in public. Nothing would stop her from going to China!

But first, she needed to acquire the necessary skills, learn Chinese, and get the financial and logistical support required for such a gargantuan undertaking. Surely, she thought, her enthusiasm and dedication would suffice to achieve all these.

Unfortunately, the China Inland Mission thought otherwise. Gladys could still hear the director's words, echoing in her head, "If you went on, it would be a waste of everyone's time and money . . ."

"I am your God . . . go!"

There was, however, "one more thing", said the director. Appreciative of her keenness to serve God, the kindly man told her about an old missionary couple who had just returned from China and needed help looking after their house in Bristol. "Would you," he asked tentatively, "be prepared to consider the job?"[7]

On hearing this, Gladys nearly broke down in tears. A housemaid's job—again! Her dream of going to China had never seemed further away. But if it was what God wanted her to do, well . . .

Glumly, she nodded and took down the address of the couple. It wasn't long, however, before she realised that this was all part of God's divine plan. While the work was anything but mission-like, Gladys found inspiration in the simple but powerful faith of the Fishers. When she shared her dreams and disappointments with them, they assured her of God's faithfulness. "God never lets you down," they told her. "He sends you, guides you, and provides for you. Maybe He doesn't answer your prayers as you want them answered, but He does answer them."[8]

But she had just been rejected, she pointed out. Was God telling her she was not meant to be a missionary? Did He still want her to go to China? The couple did not have any answers for her, except: "He will show you in His own good time. Keep on watching and praying."[9]

That "good time" came in due course. On the Fishers' recommendations, Gladys moved to Swansea in Wales to work at a rescue mission that helped young girls in trouble. Many had left their villages in search of jobs, only to end up homeless and penniless in the city. Some had turned to prostitution in desperation, and it was the job of "rescue sisters" like Gladys to persuade them to get help at the mission and to go home. It was a meaningful task, but Gladys could not get China off her mind. One day, after deciding to read the entire Bible from the beginning, she was struck by Genesis 12:1.

"Go from your country, your people and your father's household to the land I will show you," God told Abraham. Gladys' heart jumped. Was God telling her to do the same thing? On another day, she read about how Moses left the comfort and security of his desert home to lead the Israelites out of Egypt. Later, she found inspiration in Nehemiah's determination to go to Jerusalem to help his people, even though he was still serving the Persian king.

"Just like me," thought Gladys. Then she exclaimed aloud: "But he did go . . . he went in spite of everything!"

At that very moment, she seemed to hear a voice say to her, "Gladys Aylward, is Nehemiah's God your God?"

"Yes, of course!" she replied. To which she heard, "Then do what Nehemiah did, and go."

"But I am not Nehemiah," she countered.

"No, but assuredly, I am his God."[10]

That was it. Gladys knew that she had just received her "marching orders" to go to China. Now, all that was left was the question of how to get there.

Aware of the need to grow her savings, she moved back to London, where the employment agency sent her to the home of Francis Younghusband, the famous explorer who had led expeditions to Central Asia and China. Spending almost the last of her money on the train ticket to get there, she went to her room, laid her Bible, a devotional book, and her remaining 2½ pennies on the bed. Then she prayed simply, "God, here's the Bible about which I long to tell others, here's everything I have. If you want me, I am going to China with these."[11]

No sooner were the words out of her mouth when she was summoned to see the mistress of the house. The kindly lady told her it was her practice to reimburse new maids for their transport, and gave her three shillings—even more than she had spent on the train fare. Clutching it tightly, she went back upstairs in awe. God had just showed her He would provide!

Strengthened by the little miracle, Gladys went down to the travel agent as soon as she could to book passage on a ship to China. She was dismayed to find out that the cheapest fare was £90, far more than she could ever dream of saving. There was a slightly more affordable alternative—an arduous 5,000-mile journey overland on the Trans-Siberian Railway through Holland, Germany, Poland, Russia, and Siberia, followed by a ship to China. It would take several weeks and cost just under £48.

But there was a snag: the railway passed through what was now a conflict zone. An undeclared war was raging at the Sino-Russian border, she was told, and the fighting threatened the train line. Gladys dismissed the travel agent's warnings and asked him to book a ticket immediately. She would pay three pounds as a deposit now, she said, and follow up with instalments every week. "I couldn't really care about a silly old war," she said airily. "It'll be all over by the time I get the rest of the money, I'm sure."

The agent refused to sell her the ticket. "We do not like to deliver our customers dead," he protested vehemently. But Gladys insisted, and the booking was made.[12]

Having won this small victory and taken the first of many steps to China, Gladys got her head down and began to save as much money as she could, taking on extra jobs as a kitchen helper, cleaner, and waitress, and selling whatever belongings she had, including her best pair of shoes. "It's all for China," she reminded herself constantly.[13] God added to her savings along the way, giving her little "bonuses". As a result, Gladys managed to pay the full train fare within a year instead of the three she had calculated. God had given her an extra two years to serve Him in China.

The next step was to figure out what she would do when she actually got to China. One day, she overheard a friend's conversation about a 73-year-old missionary stationed in China who needed "some younger woman" to carry on her work. Gladys' eyes widened. "That's meant for me, all right," she said to herself.[14] The Fishers were right: God was revealing His plans for her, in His own time.

She wrote to the woman, Jeannie Lawson, and after a seemingly interminable wait, received the reply: yes, Jeannie needed help to keep her mission going in the city of Yangcheng (Jincheng city today) in Shanxi province, but Gladys had to find her own way there.

So on 15 October 1932, armed with her Bible, a fountain pen, some warm clothing weighing a little over two pounds, and food for the long journey—knowing she could not afford to buy any along the way—Gladys boarded the train at Liverpool Street station and set off for China. It was, as biographer Alan Burgess put it, probably one of "the most ill-equipped expeditions ever to leave the shores of England".[15] But of this Gladys was sure: it was God who was sending her to China, and He would provide for, protect, and guide her, just as He had Abraham, Moses, and Nehemiah.

The Inn of Eight Happinesses

The story of how Gladys got to China and what she did there has been recounted in many books and even featured in a movie. It is a dramatic account that can easily distract readers from the impact that she made on the people she ministered to. Yet both attest to God's power and might, and show how He could use someone like Gladys so mightily.

The journey from London to China was a miracle in itself. After many days of travel, the train came to a halt in the middle of Siberia; fighting ahead had made it impossible to continue. Gladys had to walk for more than a day to the nearest town, from where she managed to make her way to Vladivostok on the eastern coast. There, she was accosted—and nearly raped—by a Russian official who kept her passport and tried to trick her into staying on in the country to work as a machinist. An English-speaking woman appeared out of nowhere and arranged for her to escape on a ship to Japan. In Kobe, she was led to an English missionary couple who helped her board another ship to China. On 8 November, Gladys finally set foot in the land she had long dreamt of serving God in. It marked the beginning of 17 exciting, drama-filled years of ministry.

In the city of Yangcheng in northern China, Gladys and Jeannie faced strong resistance to the gospel. Steeped in their traditional beliefs and culture, villagers had little time for the "foreign devils" and their so-called "good news". But the two women came up with a brilliant plan: set up an overnight stopover for the passing traders who transported their goods via "trains" of burden-bearing mules, and entertain them with stories at dinnertime as an incentive to stay on.

The Inn of Eight Happinesses—the number eight being considered auspicious in Chinese culture—soon became known for its entertaining tales, told in dramatic fashion by the two foreign women and their Chinese workers who had converted to Christianity. These stories told of a middle-eastern man called Jesus whose honourable ancestor was the great God, how he lived in a simple society, and how he overcame his problems. These were stories the mule drivers could identify with, and they were so intriguing that they began to tell them to others, thus multiplying the missionaries' efforts to spread the gospel throughout the isolated, mountainous region.

At first, lacking the language skills, Gladys could only perform the tack of running out to grab the first animal of each passing mule caravan and pull it in, forcing the rest to follow, and then feeding and cleaning the dirty mules. Slowly, however, she picked up the Shanxi dialect and was able to join her colleague on forays to the countryside to tell these stories in villages. But when Jeannie passed away after a fall, Gladys faced her first major test: with no more money coming from Jeannie's pension, how was she going to continue running the inn?

God's solution came in the unlikely form of the Mandarin of Yangcheng, the city's governor, who wanted Gladys to be his "foot inspector". The Chinese government was trying to end the age-old tradition of binding girls' feet—which was believed to make them more attractive—and needed officials to enforce a new law against the practice. Gladys, who had "big" feet by local standards, was deemed the perfect candidate for inspecting girls' feet and explaining why foot-binding was unhealthy and cruel.

At first, Gladys recoiled. She had come all the way to China to tell the good news—not to inspect feet! Then she realised that God had given her the perfect opportunity to be His witness. The job would give her official authority to tour the villages, along with some payment, mules for transport, and even two bodyguards. When she warned the Mandarin that she would also evangelise to the people she met, he waved it off. "I care nothing for your religion or to whom you preach. This is a matter for the conscience of each individual," he replied—thus giving Gladys the green light to preach.[16]

This she did, combining her foot inspections with stories about Jesus during the day, followed by more stories at the Inn of Eight Happinesses in the evenings. One by one, souls were won for

Christ as people began to turn to Jesus as their Lord and Saviour. Some became her lifelong friends and helpers in her ministry.

Gladys' gentle demeanour and compassionate bearing also won her acceptance among the locals, and soon, she had so impressed the Mandarin that when a riot broke out in a local prison, he summoned her to quell it. The prisoners had run amok, the prison governor told her, and were killing each other. It had become so violent that even the soldiers dared not enter the prison grounds. "You must go in and stop the fighting," he said.

Gladys' eyes widened. "Are you mad!" she protested. "If I went in they'd kill me!"

"But how can they kill you?" the governor retorted. "You tell everybody that you have come here because you have the living God inside you. If you preach the truth, if your God protects you from harm, then you can stop this riot."

With the reputation of God at stake, Gladys had no choice but to walk into the prison unaccompanied. There, a shocking spectacle greeted her. The inmates were fighting, and one man was running around with an axe. Bodies of several of his victims lay on the ground. The man headed for her, but somehow, Gladys found the courage to stand her ground. "Give me that chopper!" she demanded. "Give it to me at once!"[17]

To her surprise—and that of the other inmates—the man complied. Like a schoolteacher telling off a class of naughty kids, she then ordered them to get in line and explain their behaviour. That's when she found out that the prisoners had rioted because of the poor conditions they faced: they had little to eat, little opportunity for exercise, and nothing to do. She brought this up to the prison authorities, convinced them to improve the conditions, and got them to set up looms and a grindstone so that the men could weave cloth and grind grain, both for themselves and to sell. She also began to visit them and preach to them. A number of criminals were converted, and one of them, Feng, even became a stalwart supporter in her ministry.

The incident sealed Gladys' reputation around the countryside. They began to call her "Ai Wei De"—a Chinese rendition of her name that also meant "Virtuous One". To the English native who had given up everything she had to come to this foreign country, being treated like a fellow Chinese was the highest accolade she could receive. In 1935, Gladys decided to give up her British passport and become a Chinese citizen. In a letter to her family back home, she said, "This is indeed my country and these are my people. I live now completely as a Chinese woman. I wear their clothes, eat their food, speak their language—even their dialect— and I am thinking like they do."[18]

The Mandarin, too, was greatly moved by Gladys' faith and actions. Over the years and over the course of many conversations about their differing culture and faith, he and Gladys had come to a mutual understanding. One day, at a banquet, he praised the missionary for her work among the poor, the sick, and the prisoners. Then he announced solemnly, "I would like to embrace your faith, Ai-weh-deh. I would like to become a Christian!"[19]

A Long Walk to Safety

By this time, Gladys had also started to take in unwanted and orphaned children. It started with a beggar woman offering to sell her daughter to her; filled with compassion and knowing that she could give the girl better care, Gladys gave the woman all the money she had on her—the equivalent of nine pennies—and adopted the child. She named the child Mei-en ("Grace") but called her by her nickname, Ninepence. One day, the girl brought back another homeless child, and he was followed by another and yet another. Over the next few years, the Inn of Eight Happinesses became an orphanage of sorts, which prompted the provincial governor to start a school. If Gladys had ever fretted over not being a mother, she now had more children than she could ever have dreamed of.

In 1937, the happy state of affairs was disrupted by war erupting between China and Japan. Air raids by Japanese planes destroyed Yangcheng as well as Gladys' inn, and successive advances by Japanese troops left the missionary convinced that she had to leave the city. Her life was also in danger because she had helped the defending Nationalist Army by reporting the movements of Japanese troops while travelling around the region as a missionary; as a result, the Japanese had put a price on her head. The question was: how was she going to ensure the safety of the 100 children under her charge?

The answer that came was a challenging one. Gladys heard that the wife of the Nationalist leader, Madam Chiang Kai Shek, had set up a shelter for children orphaned by the war. But the home was in the city of Sian (Xi'an today) to the west, more than 200 kilometres away and separated from Yangcheng by both mountains and the Yellow River. Gladys had no other means of getting the children—some of whom were still infants—across; they simply had to walk.

And so, in April 1940, the missionary and her 100 children set off, each of them equipped with little more than a small bowl, chopsticks, a towel, and some kind of quilt to sleep on. Over two weeks, they saw the grace of God first-hand as He protected them from the weather, snakes, and Japanese troops. They also saw His constant provision at work in the form of friendly soldiers who shared their meagre rations, a Buddhist monk who housed them in an abandoned temple, and an officer who ordered boats to take them across the Yellow River even though it was officially closed off. All in all, it took them about a month to reach Sian. It was a death-defying trek that testified to God's greatness. Although the long walk to safety left Gladys ill from typhoid fever, she had not lost a single child.

The tireless missionary, however, was back at work the moment she recovered. Unable to return to Yangcheng, she stayed on in

Sian, where she ministered to war refugees, lepers, and prisoners, and continued going into the mountains to preach to villagers. It was tiring, but God encouraged Gladys constantly with reminders of the importance of her work. Once, when she visited an isolated monastery, she was surprised to find the inhabitants ready to accept her message of the gospel. "Here at long last is the messenger we have waited for," they told her.[20]

She later moved to Chengdu in the south, where she spent another four years caring for the needy, preaching the good news, and teaching the Bible. She also took on a key teaching role at a theological seminary that was usually reserved for Chinese women—she had become so naturalised that she was now considered a fellow Chinese.

Following the Communist takeover of China, Gladys returned to England in 1949. For the next 10 years, she taught children at a school and shared her testimony repeatedly to raise funds for mission work in China. But she could not get China off her mind; it had become her true home, and she yearned greatly to return. She was denied re-entry by the new Chinese government, however, and decided to settle in Taiwan, where she set up an orphanage and spent her last years caring for more children.

By the time Gladys died on 3 January 1970, she was famous. Numerous magazine articles and books had been written about her dramatic escape through the mountains and her other exploits in China. Her adventures were even turned into a movie, which embarrassed her with its somewhat distorted account of her life. Still, the fame that the publicity brought her was useful, as it helped her to raise more funds for the country she loved.

All this was most ironic, given that she had once failed her language and theology examinations, and was told that she was too old to become a missionary. Gladys never blamed the missions agency for rejecting her. "I know, if no one else does, how stupid I must have seemed then," she admitted once. "The fact that I learned not only to speak, but also to read and write the Chinese language like a native in later years, is to me one of God's great miracles."[21]

And while she had never wavered in her determination to serve God in China and her passion for her ministry never waned, she always remained grateful for the opportunity to see God's provision up close. In fact, she even expressed surprise at being called by Him to do His work in China. "I wasn't God's first choice for what I've done for China," she said frankly. "I don't know who it was. It must have been a man—a well-educated man. I don't know what happened. Perhaps he died. Perhaps he wasn't willing. And God looked down . . . and saw Gladys Aylward. And God said, 'Well, she's willing.'"[22]

Six

The Difficult Visitors
Ludwig Ingwer Nommensen

Ludwig Ingwer Nommensen (1834–1918) was a German missionary who spent more than half his life working with the ethnic Batak on the Indonesian island of Sumatra. Over more than 50 years, God sustained him through persecution and personal tragedies in the valley of Silindung, bringing the gospel to tribes who had not heard of Jesus Christ. Through godly words and actions, Ludwig showed God's love to the Batak and converted thousands to the Christian faith. Today, the Batak church is one of the largest church denominations in Indonesia, and much of its success can be traced to the man many have called the Apostle to the Batak.

They came in the morning, darkening the doorway of the simple hut as they filed in one by one, purposeful and aggressive. There were six of them, and they meant business. The chiefs of the Batak village had shown themselves capable of violence, unafraid to do harm if they felt it would serve their needs.

Startled, Ludwig Ingwer Nommensen took a step back. The German missionary had become accustomed to hostility ever since he started working among the Batak in the valley of Silindung on Sumatra, but he wasn't sure what travails these men would bring today. Were they here to ask more probing questions about his faith, to demand compensation for some supposed misdeed of his, or simply to threaten him physically?

Ludwig had no illusions about what the Batak were capable of. The culture of many indigenous tribes in the Dutch East Indies (now Indonesia) embraced cannibalism, and two pioneering American missionaries sent there many years ago had been killed and eaten. Attempts had also been made to poison Ludwig several times, and each time, God had delivered him—miraculously—from danger.

The six men, however, showed no signs that they were about to do Ludwig any personal harm. They began by asking the same questions they had been throwing at him since he arrived in 1862. Some of these questions were born of curiosity, some were meant to test him, and some were just plain threats. "Where is your land?" "Where do heaven and earth meet?" "When are you leaving?"[1]

With as much patience as he could muster, Ludwig tried to answer them reasonably. The Batak had shown great capacity for intellectual argument, and had kept him on the tip of his mental toes as they challenged the tenets of his faith. This time, however, the chiefs weren't listening. Today, they were here simply to harass him. Tiring of the questioning, they then demanded that the missionary entertain them.

Knowing that he could not afford to offend the chiefs, who were highly respected by the villagers, Ludwig showed them his watch and photographs of his family and homeland, played the violin, and even demonstrated how his magnifying glass—which they had never seen before—worked. When lunchtime came, he offered them a simple meal, which they wolfed down without hesitation.

But it still wasn't enough. The chiefs clearly wanted to provoke Ludwig. Perhaps they were hoping he would lose his patience and give them an excuse to sneer at his supposed religion of peace. Ludwig had thrown out an intruder once, and still felt a pang of shame for losing his cool. Or, perhaps they were hoping that he would finally tire of the constant pestering, and leave the village once and for all. This thought made the missionary even more determined to put up with his boisterous visitors—even when one of them went into his bedroom uninvited and spat on the floor to express his contempt. His deep blue eyes twinkling, Ludwig simply gave them his gentle smile, as if it didn't bother him.

The men then tried more specific threats. "We will chop off your feet and throw you into the river," one said. To which Ludwig replied equably, "Ah, my friend, you do not mean that at all." "If you try to build a house, we will burn it down," another said. "Then I will build it again," countered Ludwig. This went on, back and forth, until it was afternoon.[2]

Yawning, the chiefs announced that they needed a nap. Ludwig hoped that they were planning to leave. But no! The six men just stretched out on the wooden floor and went to sleep. Ludwig sighed and tried to tidy up the house as they snored. When the men woke up, Ludwig told them some Bible stories. The men listened with some interest, interrupting at times with acid comments, and then asked more pointless questions. By now, it was dark, and the missionary was tired. Not once had he given any indication of his own impatience, but the chiefs showed no sign of letting up in this clash of wills.

Finally, at around midnight, Ludwig couldn't stay up any longer. While he wasn't comfortable with having six aggressive men staying overnight, he couldn't keep his eyes open for much more. "I am exhausted," he told them. "I have to sleep."[3]

The six men looked at each other. If the foreigner was going to sleep, well, they would too! One nodded at the others, as if to say, "Let's see how long he can keep this up." Again, they lay down to sleep where they sat. Ludwig retired to his bedroom and, getting on his knees, prayed for more patience and compassion for the people God had sent him to. If this was indeed God's will, he prayed, six persistent chiefs were not going to deter him from ministering to the Batak. Then he too went to sleep.

The next morning, when the chiefs woke up, it was cool. In the interior of Sumatra, it was not uncommon for the air to turn chilly in the early hours. The six men were surprised to find that atop each of them lay a warm, woollen blanket. Evidently, sometime during the night, the man they had tormented for an entire day had woken up and covered them with the blankets. The Batak chiefs looked at each other with embarrassment. For all the trouble they had given Ludwig, he had seen it fit to treat them as honoured guests, returning their hostility and rudeness with the greatest kindness and compassion.

Quietly, trying not to wake their host up, the chiefs folded up their blankets, placed them neatly on a table, and left Ludwig's house in silence.

This incident was not forgotten by the Batak chiefs. Many years later, one of them would recount it to Ludwig, acknowledging the impression the patient missionary had made on them. Along with his other efforts, the man said, it had helped to change their attitude towards the gospel he was preaching. Ludwig chuckled and told his apologetic listener that he was forgiven. After all, he added, that was what his mission was all about when he came to the Batak of Silindung: to preach peace and forgiveness from Jesus Christ.

In a way, that day with the Batak chiefs also captured Ludwig's ministry to the Batak in a nutshell. Throughout much of the 50-plus years in Sumatra, Ludwig faced great opposition to the gospel, but never once let it stop him from witnessing for Christ. Like the apostle Paul, he counted it an honour to suffer for the sake of his Lord. It spoke of the patience, determination, and faith that had sustained him from young and brought him to the valley of Silindung.

A "Miracle" Healing

Born 6 February 1834 into a poor family on the island of Nordstrand in Schleswig-Holstein district—now part of Germany but then under the control of Denmark—Ludwig was expected to work as soon as he was old enough. At seven, he began earning money by tending geese and sheep. An accident at age twelve nearly put an end to his useful life. While playing one day, he somehow fell under the wheels of a horse cart which rolled over both his legs, crushing them. It seemed that he would never walk again: a year later, Ludwig was still bedridden. Visiting doctors did their best, but he didn't respond to their treatments.

His parents, who were devout Christians, kept assuring Ludwig that he would walk again one day, but looking at his frail legs, the thirteen-year-old found this hard to believe. One Christmas, while reading his Bible, he came across John 14:14: "You may ask me for anything in my name, and I will do it." Trembling, he asked his mother, "Is this true? Do miracles still happen today?"[4]

Ludwig's mother hesitated. The doctors had expressed doubt that her son's legs would ever recover fully, but she couldn't bear to disappoint her dear son. Trying to look confident, she smiled and replied, "Of course, dear. It's true because that's God's Word."

For Ludwig, that answer was good enough. If his mother said so, then it had to be true! For the first time in many months, he felt the assurance of hope as he began to ask God to heal his legs. If he could walk again, he vowed, he would become a missionary. Ludwig believed that if God gave him his legs back, it would be for a specific purpose.

God's answer, as far as Ludwig was concerned, came soon after. Sometime after he began to pray for healing, a doctor who occasionally checked on him prescribed a new medicine, and his wounds began to heal. A year or so later, he was walking normally. Ludwig had no doubt that God's hand was behind his healing and didn't forget his vow. Walking into a church one day, he got down on his knees, thanked God, and asked Him, "Do You want me to become a missionary?"

While no voices rang in his head and no Bible verse came to mind, Ludwig felt convinced that God had replied, "Yes."

While Ludwig was ready to respond immediately, he had to undergo several tests of his patience and determination. First, his father died, so he had to continue working to support the family. Only after his oldest sister married and could take over his role was he able to enrol at the Rhenish Mission Society. There, he faced a brief test. Arriving at the mission house, he was given a cold welcome by the inspector because he had turned up before being officially summoned. Made to stand at the man's office door for two hours and be studiously ignored, Ludwig waited patiently. That impressed the inspector, who later said of the young man: "Who can wait patiently for two hours without being offended, can surely do more."[5]

That enduring patience would turn out to be one of Ludwig's greatest strengths.

Around 1859, Ludwig began to hear about the need for God's messengers in Borneo and Sumatra, two large islands that were part of the Dutch colony in Southeast Asia. Several missionaries sent to Borneo had made some headway, but a violent revolt by the natives had broken out, killing several and forcing the others to evacuate. Some of the missionaries had fled to Sumatra, where they saw a potential mission field among the native Batak.

The reports inspired Ludwig, who had long been wondering where God would send him. "Before this I have had little ambition to go to Borneo, but now all the more," he wrote in a letter to friends.[6] "The blood of the brethren is crying over to us, to you, to all Christendom. This blood is the seed for Borneo, which will bring forth fruit a hundredfold."

After being ordained in 1861, Ludwig put in a request to be sent to the Batak in Sumatra. It was quickly approved, and after undergoing some language lessons in Holland, he was on his way.

From Europe to Silindung

Arriving in the coastal town of Padang in western Sumatra on 14 May 1862, after a four-month journey prolonged by windless seas, Ludwig took in his first sight of the tropics and culture of Sumatra—and immediately came up against the same obstacles that fellow missionaries were facing in their ministry. The Dutch colonial authorities had placed strict restrictions on their movement, not allowing the missionaries to enter the interior of the island or settle in certain areas. Some of the rules were ostensibly established for their safety, as the Batak priest-king Sisingamangaraja XI and his son were locked in a guerrilla war against colonial rule.

Unable to move into the interior, Ludwig spent a few years along the coast, learning the Batak language and Malay, adapting to the tropics, and interacting with the locals. It turned out to be a productive time, for it helped to cement the missionary's belief that eventually he would have to train up natives to reach out to their own people. Ultimately, he saw, a foreign missionary could not make the same inroads into people's hearts and lives that a local one could.

In line with this belief, Ludwig determined to live and think like a Sumatran. He even changed his diet, eschewing European food for a spartan diet of rice, dried fish, and vegetables. Interacting with natives holding traditional beliefs and faiths, he also learnt not to offend or confront them about their views, but instead to point out the truths of the Christian faith. He would raise a discussion on sin, for example, and ask, "Who pays your debt of sin?"[7]

But he never lost sight of his ultimate goal: witnessing to the Batak. Despite the restrictions, he made several forays into the interior, visiting missionaries and scouting around for a suitable base. This he found in the beautiful, isolated valley of Silindung, tucked away in the mountain ridges around Lake Toba. It was a fertile area inhabited by thousands of Batak, most of whom had little contact with the outside world. This, Ludwig determined, was where he would begin God's ministry.

An Unfriendly Welcome

One of the largest indigenous groups in Sumatra, the Batak was in fact made up of several closely-related ethnic groups. They included the Toba, Simalungun, Karo, Dairi, Angkola, and Mandailing. Traditionally followers of ancestral worship and animism, they venerated the many gods and spirits that they believed lived in plants, trees, and nature, and offered sacrifices to ancestors. Rituals, sorcery, and occult spells were an integral part of their lives—as was cannibalism, which sealed their reputation as fearsome warriors. Defeated enemies were ritually eaten after being offered as sacrifices.

The Batak around Toba lived in a constant state of war. Divided into smaller tribes and villages, they regularly fought among themselves. The clashes were rooted in a strong tribal and clan identity that all Batak possessed, and which was also expressed in a deep suspicion of all outsiders. This especially included missionaries, who were not only associated with the Dutch colonisers, but also seen as a threat to Batak traditional culture and customs. When Ludwig set up a school, for instance, they kept their children away. When he explained that he was there to show them how to become wise and happy, they retorted that they were wise and happy enough.

Within days of settling in Silindung, Ludwig began to face strong opposition from those he was attempting to reach out to, which was followed by constant persecution. In his characteristic manner, he bore all these with great equanimity. God not only gave him the strength, patience, and wisdom to deal with the challenges, but also protected him divinely.

When Ludwig was building a shelter for converts ostracised by their families, villagers came to disrupt the construction, sabotaging it and demanding ransoms for tools and materials which they grabbed from the builders. With great presence of mind, Ludwig calmly went to the village chiefs and offered to take note of their names; this scared off the superstitious Batak, who believed this would give the white man power over them.

Numerous attempts were made on his life. A native, over several nights, loosened the ropes holding the missionary's ramshackle wooden home together, so that it would collapse on him. But one evening, an earthquake drove Ludwig out of the hut—just before it collapsed to the ground. Twice he was administered poison, but nothing happened to him. This frightened the perpetrators into thinking that he was a great sorcerer. Later, they confessed their crime to Ludwig, who readily forgave them. Both became Christians.

Another time, Ludwig was to attend an important traditional festival involving Batak from different tribes and villages. Wisely, he had written to a number of tribal chiefs and persuaded them to keep the peace at this event. At the festival, however, a supposed medium for an ancestral spirit announced that the spirit demanded a human sacrifice; it was clearly directed at Ludwig.

Before a riot could break out, the missionary stood up and pointed out that this had to be the devil's plot, for no ancestor would want a human sacrifice, just as no grandfather would desire the death of his grandchild. His convincing words calmed the crowd down. But the next day, some tribal enemies stirred up the crowds again, and fighting broke out, wounding one man. Just as the situation threatened to blow up, a sudden storm swept through the area. The thunder and lightning not only broke up the fighting, but also convinced the Batak that the missionary's God was powerful indeed.

In letters to friends, Ludwig explained that he saw no reason to fear the attempts on his life. Surely, he reasoned, God would not let anything happen to him after healing his wounds and bringing him so far to proclaim the gospel to the Batak. "It is God who supplies me with ever new courage and strength, that I have not yet let my hands sink exhausted," he said.[8]

Thus, Ludwig continued to share the good news of Jesus, holding long discussions with villagers about God and beginning translation of the Bible and other teaching materials into the Batak language. Knowing that the natives loved storytelling, he taught the Bible through stories they could identify with. For example, he would portray Christ's work of redemption as a battle between God's goodness and the work of devil; this was readily understood by listeners used to warfare. He also encouraged converts to "gossip" about the gospel to their family and friends.

At the same time, Ludwig also did his best to improve the lives of the Batak. He coaxed parents to let their children attend his little school to learn practical skills in subjects such as math and basic hygiene. He also applied what little he knew of Western medicine to the ill, introduced vaccination to ward off smallpox, and mediated between warring chiefs.

What really made his ministry effective was his determination to embrace the Batak lifestyle, his sensitivity to their traditions, and his belief that Christian practices could be adapted to their social norms and culture where they did not clash with Christian doctrine. He took care not to impose a European culture onto the native church, avoided preaching at their religious festivals, and encouraged them to retain traditional customs unless they were related to witchcraft and sorcery.

Ludwig had great respect for the Batak social order, called *adat*, which was based on social and clan hierarchies and expressed in their customs, rituals, and everyday behaviour. Whether he was evangelising to unreached communities or setting up a local church, he would follow the Batak approach to relationships and organisation. This included giving special recognition and respect to tribal chiefs, whose position was held in the highest regard by all Batak. When several local chiefs converted to Christianity, it gave Ludwig's ministry an added boost, for the leaders would convince the villagers to follow suit.

The Birth of the Batak Church

Thanks to Ludwig's perseverance, his ministry began to see results. In August 1865, he baptised his first converts—four men and their wives and children. Over the following months, this number grew slowly but steadily. It was not an easy decision for the Batak converts: many were thrown out of their homes, ostracised by their clans, or continually attacked for abandoning their traditional beliefs. As a result, they lost their place in society and their livelihoods.

At first, Ludwig sheltered some in his home and a mission station he had set up, but when the number of converts passed 1,000, and then 2,000, this became challenging. So, around 1869, the mission station was remodelled into a Christian village which he called Huta Dame, or Village of Peace. Here, the converts could live with fellow Christians, grow their crops, and worship together in a new church that was erected.

This, however, did not mean the end of persecution. In the Village of Peace, Ludwig and the converts found themselves under continued and constant attack. Enemies harassed them during their services, disturbed women in the fields, picked quarrels with church leaders and demanded money, shot and killed several believers, and incited other tribal chiefs to attack Huta Dame. At one time, the priest-king Sisingamangaraja XII declared war on the village, prompting Ludwig and fellow missionary Peter Johanssen, who had been sent to support him, to prepare for the worst.

"May the Lord prepare us rightly, so that we may be ready to glorify His name in our death," Ludwig wrote to the assistant inspector of the Rhenish Missionary Society back home. And, as always, forgiveness and the Lord's mission dominated his mind and heart. "Avenge our blood by sending out flocks of messengers of peace," he added, "whose feet are beautiful in the mountains to proclaim peace, that the poor nation may learn to know its Saviour."[9]

Once again, God intervened to preserve His missionary and the fledgling church. A quarrel broke out among the tribal chiefs, distracting them from the problem of Huta Dame. This was followed by a smallpox epidemic, which dissuaded them from entering the area. Typically, Ludwig saw the good in everything. While wars were dangerous, he observed, they could also lead to villagers seeing the value of the peace that could be found in Jesus. "So we also hope for something good out of the wars of the Batak, and believe that we are not mistaken," he concluded.[10]

He was not mistaken. By the turn of the century, entire Batak tribes and villages had converted to Christianity, and the small church Ludwig had established in Silindung had become a full-fledged indigenous church, with its own order and hierarchy. It had also expanded significantly to include "branches" in other areas around Lake Toba, a theological seminary that trained local pastors, and a mission society that reached out to other Batak tribes.

Ludwig's Legacy

When the Batak church celebrated the fiftieth anniversary of the mission on 7 October 1911, the celebrations in the market area of Sitahuru—where Ludwig was once meant to be sacrificed—drew about 12,000 Christians. It was just a fraction of the number of converts that the mission had seen over the past five decades. As joyful missionaries and converts recounted and reflected on the ordeal of the early days, they praised God for the amazing fact that Silindung was now home to more than 100,000 Christians. Significantly, the church was truly a native one: it had over 2,000 Batak leaders, including nearly 30 pastors and 700 teachers, 26 evangelists, and 1,500 elders.

As the 77-year-old "bishop" of the church—Ludwig—watched the proceedings and smiled, he thought about how God had enabled him to overcome opposition and persecution through the years in Sumatra. He had needed every bit of God's comfort and strength, especially when facing the deaths of two wives and four children during this time.

His first wife, Karoline Gutbrod, whom he married in 1866, died in 1887. This came after the deaths of two of their six children. In 1892, Ludwig married Anna Christine Harder and they had three children. Nine years later, another son from his first marriage was brutally murdered in Sumatra, while Anna died in 1909. Another son from his second marriage would die fighting in World War I.

Ludwig himself was called home to the Lord on 23 May 1918. By then, the Batak church had more than 180,000 members led by over 30 pastors and some 800 teacher-preachers.

Today, the Batak church is one of the largest church denominations in Southeast Asia. The Huria Kristen Batak Protestan Church, or

Batak Christian Protestant Church, is part of the Lutheran World Federation and is said to number more than 4 million.

Ludwig himself has been hailed by some historians as one of the greatest modern-day missionaries ever. But his legacy should go beyond the numbers; what makes him stand out is his enduring faith and unshakeable belief in God's love for all men. This compelled him to reach out to a people who had not only continually resisted his efforts but even tried to kill him on several occasions. From putting up with six hostile tribal chiefs to preaching the gospel in the face of constant threats to his life, Ludwig Nommensen displayed and shared the perfect love, everlasting forgiveness, and matchless compassion of God.

Seven

An Indefinite Plan
Sophia Blackmore

Sophia Blackmore (1857–1945), the first woman missionary sent by the Methodist Women's Foreign Missionary Society to Singapore, devoted her life not only to sharing the gospel but also to improving the livelihoods of people she reached out to. Overcoming prejudice against women and the education of girls, she set up two schools and a boarding home for girls, and helped to lay the foundations for a new church. Throughout her mission, God guided her path, opened doors, and gave her the persistence and strength to overcome cultural barriers and traditional prejudices to share His love.

Sophia Blackmore's worst fears seemed to be coming true. Here she was in India, thousands of miles from home, having dedicated her life to mission work. The harvest was ripe—millions of people had yet to hear of Jesus Christ, and there were just a handful of workers for the Lord. She should have had her hands full from the moment she landed.

Yet there was nothing to do. Even though Sophia was prepared to do anything, there seemed to be no appropriate role for the fresh-faced missionary from Australia. She wondered if it had anything to do with her marital status and gender. When Sophia first said yes to becoming a missionary and to leaving her home for wherever the Lord directed her, it seemed that she was ahead of her time. For the conservative church in her hometown, the idea of sending a single woman out as a missionary was virtually unthinkable. "It's just not done" seemed to be the common response she received from those who had heard of her decision.

Thus, she had had to go under the auspices of the Women's Foreign Missionary Society of the American Methodist Episcopal Church, an organisation she knew little about. The group was based on the other side of the world, and her only contact with it was through Miss Isabella Leonard, the American evangelist who had inspired her to give her life to the service of the Lord. Miss Leonard had said that there would be "plenty of work" for her in India, but could not promise if the missionary society would take her under its wing. At the time, Sophia baulked at the idea of seeking support from an organisation she had hardly heard of.

"Could it be that God wanted me to go in this indefinite way?" she asked herself. "Must I force myself among strangers? How preposterous."[1]

Remembering her promise to God to follow His will, however, she agreed. If God wanted her to go in this indefinite way, well, she would obey! Now, as she waited in India for His guidance, she held on to the memory of how God had encouraged her just months earlier. After discussing the issue with a friend, she had left the meeting convinced that God had set His seal on her decision, and she could feel His presence.

Sophia knew that in India—or wherever God would send her— her patience, obedience, and faith would be tested. So, she waited.

"Sophia is free to serve"

Born on 18 October 1857 into a devout family in Goulburn, New South Wales, Australia, Sophia was exposed to missionary life and work from young. She heard many stories from her mother, whose family had been connected to famous missionaries such as Robert Morrison, Robert Moffat, and David Livingstone.

Then came her turn to meet a real-life missionary. As a girl, Sophia was sent to stay with her mother's friend. There, she met an American evangelist—Miss Leonard—who had come to speak

at her church. "The strangeness of it frightened me", Sophia
would recall later. Some of the more conservative church-goers
would have agreed, for the idea of a woman speaking in public
was almost unheard of at the time. But many who heard Miss
Leonard speak, including Sophia's brother Hugh, were enthralled
by her teaching on sanctification.

When they met, the veteran evangelist asked the young woman
how long she had been a Christian, and then said, "Seek all Christ
has for you."[2]

Those simple words struck Sophia deeply. For the next few days,
she couldn't get them out of her mind. Concerned at how disturbed
and uneasy she looked, Sophia's mother said, "The meetings are
affecting Sophie too much; she must stay home at night."[3] But
this didn't help. A few nights later, after praying, Sophia suddenly
felt a calm assurance descend on her. It was almost as if God was
giving her His words from John 10:10 directly: "I have come that
they may have life, and have it to the full."

Sometime later, Sophia's parents moved to Sydney, but Sophia
stayed on with her mother's friend. It gave her more time with
Miss Leonard, who visited occasionally and shared inspiring
stories of the work of the Women's Foreign Missionary Society in
India. Miss Leonard said she planned to visit India herself before
returning to America. When their hostess passed away, she wrote
to Sophia and asked her point-blank: Would you like to go to
India?

The evangelist would later say that she had seen in the young woman "the gifts, graces, and usefulness" and "a clear call to missionary work".[4]

With little hesitation, Sophia said yes. Having taken Miss Leonard's first words to heart, she believed that God was showing her His plan for her. But she was less confident about the arrangements. As her church did not send single women out as missionaries, Sophia had to secure an appointment in the American-based Women's Foreign Missionary Society, which she did. This was soon arranged, and on 10 December 1886, Sophia left for India.

A Change in Mission

It would appear that God had laid out Sophia's path to Singapore long before she landed in India. In Madras (now Chennai), she met a Rev. William Oldham, who was there for a conference. When he heard about her, he knew instantly that God had answered his prayers for help.

Rev. Oldham, who had started a Methodist church on the tiny island of Singapore at the southern tip of the Malay Peninsula, had been in urgent need of both funding and manpower. The mission field in Southeast Asia was growing, and a woman missionary was desperately needed to work with the mothers and sisters of boys who attended his fledgling Anglo-Chinese School. For some time, his appeals to the Women's Foreign Missionary Society had gone unheard because there were so many similar calls for help. Then, a new branch of the agency in Minneapolis heard of Rev. Oldham's plea. Its secretary, Mrs Mary Nind, famously declared, "Frozen Minnesota will send the Gospel to the women of the Equator."[5]

The branch raised some \$3,000—paid by Mrs Nind herself—but there was no one available to go to Singapore. The women began an all-day prayer meeting for the Lord to send them someone.

Not long after, God did exactly that, setting up the meeting between Rev. Oldham and Sophia in Madras, thousands of miles away. Mrs Nind would later write, "God intended Miss Blackmore for Singapore."[6] Rev. Oldham immediately requested that the missionary society appoint Sophia. This, however, took some time, and Sophia had to wait in India for many weeks, wondering what her future held.

But Sophia did not spend those weeks waiting fruitlessly. Determined to make every day count, she asked for work, and got a job teaching in a girls' school in Moradabad in northern India. It was a short but meaningful time, for it allowed her to adapt to the tropical climate and a foreign culture. Some six months after she arrived in India, Sophia left for Singapore, arriving on 16 July 1887.

A Running Start

Both Miss Leonard and Mrs Hind were spot-on with their assessment: Sophia Blackmore was indeed intended for Singapore.

Within weeks, an opportunity came to start a girls' school to complement Oldham's Anglo-Chinese School. Several Tamil businessmen were seeking education for their daughters.

Jumping at the chance, Sophia began buying furniture and obtained a space in a small shophouse in the city. On 15 August, barely a month after her arrival, she launched the Tamil Girls' School. It had just nine girls, who loved the studies so much that they told Sophia they would rather go to school than go on holiday.

Sophia's second venture into education, however, had a much tougher start.

While Singapore contained an intriguing mix of races, religions, and ethnicities, a large majority of the population was Chinese. Prompted to reach out to this community, Sophia decided to set up a mission in Chinatown, where many of them lived. She began going around the neighbourhood, house by house, to share the gospel and persuade families to send their daughters to school. Like Rev. Oldham, she believed that sharing God's love included improving the livelihoods of people, and education was a key to helping them.

Many of the families in the area were Straits-born Chinese, also known as Peranakan or Baba Chinese. These were the descendants of ethnic Chinese who had emigrated from China many years ago; born in Malaya and Singapore, they had assimilated local culture and often spoke Malay, which Sophia began to learn.

At first, the missionary couldn't even find the women of the homes; they seemed to disappear whenever she called at the door. Later, she found out a rumour had been going around that the Caucasian woman was a "spy" sent by the colonial government to check on people who gambled at home; an activity outlawed at the time.

After dispelling that rumour, Sophia found herself fending off inquisitive personal questions. The women just could not understand why this young, vivacious lady wasn't married when she looked most eligible. Inevitably, their questions to her, made through an interpreter, would go along the lines of: "Where did she come from?", "Is she married?", then "How old is she?", and followed by "Why did her mother not get her married?"[7]

The questions showed Sophia the great challenge she faced in reaching out to the old-fashioned, conservative Chinese community, most of whom followed traditional religious practices and did not believe that girls needed to be educated. In their minds, a woman's place was at home, so there was no need for her to study. Sophia wasn't too surprised—she had faced similar opposition herself at home when she first became a missionary.

True enough, the parents protested. "We do not want our girls to *makan gaji* (Malay for earning one's livelihood)," said many.[8] One woman even told Sophia that if her daughter and son were to study from the same books, the girl would get all the learning and leave nothing for the boy. It was all right for girls to be stupid—but the boys had to be clever.

But Sophia persisted. She dealt with the embarrassing personal questions using her sense of humour, and continued to visit the homes. Over time, her gentle demeanour and deep sincerity began to win hearts, and residents began to invite her into their homes to hear what she had to say about her faith. One woman even offered a space in her home to start another school for the girls, an offer that Sophia took up gratefully. The Anglo-Chinese Girls' School was born. Starting with eight girls, it slowly grew as word spread about how it helped to nurture girls into becoming good wives and mothers.

Complementing the two schools was a boarding home that Sophia opened to house some of the pupils. It began when Rev. Oldham asked her to take in the sister of a boy attending the Anglo-Chinese School. Seeing the need for more girls' accommodation, Sophia turned the Deaconess Home—where the women teachers and missionaries stayed—into a boarding home. Opened in May 1890, it became a residence not just for her pupils, but also runaways, those rescued from slavery or abandoned, and orphans.

The home, later named the Nind Home after the woman who had supported Sophia's mission, had a huge impact not only on the girls, but eventually on Singapore society as well. Many of Blackmore's Girls, as its residents became known, later became missionaries and teachers.

But while Sophia spent much time building up the two schools and the home during her time in Singapore, she never forgot the most important aspect of her mission—making disciples of the Lord. "Our chief aim in our work for women and girls was not to educate them only but to let them know of Christ Jesus as their Saviour and Friend," she once wrote in a report.[9]

At the two schools, teachers taught secular subjects as well as lessons from the Bible. Girls learnt to say prayers, memorise verses from Scripture, and sing hymns. Many of them would go home and share their discoveries with their parents.

Sophia also held Sunday services in her own home, with girls from the Nind Home, boys from another home, and Christian workers. Starting with just over 20 people, the tiny congregation grew over the years into the Straits Chinese Church, one of the first Methodist churches in Singapore to use Baba Malay in services. This church eventually became Kampong Kapor Methodist Church today.

Sophia's Legacy

Throughout her time in Singapore, Sophia had to deal with conservative attitudes and prejudices that made it hard for women to succeed. Even when she was a full-fledged missionary, some male counterparts still expressed doubt about whether women should get involved in education. But others were quick to point out that God had, through Sophia, enabled the cause of Christ to advance greatly through the schools and the people she reached out to.

Her efforts in the twin fields of evangelism and education left an indelible mark on Singapore's history. Her success in getting Chinese parents to send their girls to school complemented similar efforts being made by others, paving the way for more girls' schools to be opened.

Both of Sophia's schools continue to influence lives today. The Tamil Girls' School became the Methodist Girls' School, while the Anglo-Chinese Girls' School is today Fairfield Methodist School, named after a generous American donor who helped the school acquire a new building. They continue to nurture generation after generation of students who have brought their Christian faith to all parts of society, whether in medicine, politics, commerce, or social work.

As one missionary principal noted in an article in 1920, "The question 'Does it pay' is entirely out of place here where results can be seen every day." A generation of educated Christian women, she noted, would touch civilisation "at its most vital points".[10]

Sophia retired in 1927 and returned to Australia. Before she died on 3 July 1945, she visited Singapore several times and met many of the girls whose lives she had touched and changed.

One of those girls was Ellice Handy, a former pupil and boarder of Nind Home who became the first Asian principal of the Methodist

Girls' School. She recalled how Sophia had taught them that the Bible was the "rule of life". Miss Blackmore, she said, had never missed her evening prayers with the whole school. Every Friday, every girl had to recite a verse, and Sophia would always help those who struggled, correcting them in the gentlest way when they struggled. As Ellice concluded, "She was a mother to us all."[11]

Eight

The Inadequate Leader
Oswald Sanders

When he was young, John Oswald Sanders (1902–1992) dedicated his life to missionary service. But he never made it out into the field. Instead, he became the head of a mission agency and oversaw the dispatch of thousands of missionaries. Throughout his life, Oswald often felt inadequate for the tasks and jobs he was called to perform, but God repeatedly reminded him to step out in faith, and gave him the talents, skills, and strength needed to succeed.

Oswald was, to put it plainly, incredulous. The 52-year-old simply couldn't believe what he was reading. In his hand was a letter from the council of directors overseeing the China Inland Mission (CIM), the mission agency founded by James Hudson Taylor in 1865. A General Director was needed to helm the agency, and the council felt that John Oswald Sanders, a New Zealander, was the man for the job.

Oswald—Ossie to his many friends—wondered if there had been a mistake. To be sure, he had come from a godly Christian home, was a good public speaker and preacher, and had distinguished himself as the CIM Home Director for Australia and New Zealand, overseeing missionaries dispatched from Australasia. But taking the top post in the CIM was a different matter entirely! The General Director would supervise hundreds of missionaries, many of them veterans. What would they think of Oswald, a former lawyer who had not spent a single day in the field? How could they respect a leader who hadn't even completed a missiology course? It was absurd, thought Oswald.

As if the job itself wasn't tough enough, the 90-year-old agency was also going through one of the most tumultuous times in its history. Most of its missionaries had been thrown out of China— its main mission field—following a Communist takeover, and CIM leaders were at a loss as to what they should do next. With so many concerns and options, the various directors were sharply divided. Should they redeploy missionaries to other countries in

Asia? If so, which ones? And how, when they were so unfamiliar with the region? Or, should the agency continue to focus on China, as its name suggested? And, most importantly: What was God's will for the CIM?

And to cap it all off, the agency was facing a leadership crisis of sorts. Its top post had remained vacant for three years after its former leader, Bishop Frank Houghton, had stepped down due to overwork and ill health. This had prompted a reorganisation to share the responsibilities and workload between an Overseas Director, who would supervise work in the mission field, and a General Director, who would oversee all other matters. And as the council started combing their ranks for suitable candidates, one of them had died in a plane crash.

Oswald had long anticipated this invitation. Some time back, it had been proposed that one of the Home Directors—of which he was one—should take the top post, as they were better suited to the role than Field Directors. Alarmed, Oswald had quickly removed himself from consideration.

It wasn't the first time, however, that he had faced such a terrifying prospect. On several occasions before, Oswald had been asked to take on roles and responsibilities that were far beyond what he felt capable of. But then he remembered that each time, after he had taken the initial step of faith and obedience—and only after— God had given him the strength needed for the job. Did God intend to do the same this time?

As absurd as the council's invitation appeared, Oswald had to accept that it was composed of godly men who would not have made such a decision without extensive prayer and deliberation. The least he could do was to give it careful thought and prayer too, so that he could give them a measured response.

Over the next few days, Oswald spent much time praying over the invitation and discussing it with his wife, Edith. She was still in Australia, where they were now based, and he was in New Zealand. Writing to each other, they discussed the implications of the appointment for themselves, their teenage son Wilbur, and their extended families. As they did, Oswald developed a growing conviction that God wanted him to take the post—even though he really, really didn't want to.

Edith seemed to feel the same way about the matter. She wrote: "You know how little I want you to undertake this responsibility, but the more I pray over it, the more I feel it is inevitable and that you will have to accept it."[1]

It wasn't a pleasant feeling. Oswald felt totally inadequate for the task—more than he had ever felt in his 52 years of life. It was also a little ironic: he was being asked to head a mission agency instead of becoming a missionary himself, something he had dedicated himself towards since he was a young man. Was this really God's plan for him?

Prepared from Young

That promise to God had come more than 30 years ago, just before Oswald turned 20. Born into a devout Brethren family on 17 October 1902, John Oswald Sanders had a happy childhood growing up in Invercargill, New Zealand. His parents not only taught him and his two elder siblings, Sandy and Rita, to pray, sing hymns, and read the Bible, but also exposed them to missions when they hosted visiting missionaries. In 1921, while attending a conference, Oswald dedicated himself to missionary service after experiencing an "almost overwhelming sense of God".[2] But he would not find himself fulfilling that vow until much later.

At the age of 15, Oswald went to work as a clerk in a law firm. When his employer became ill, he took on much of the latter's work and responsibilities while studying part-time for a law degree. Impressed, his employer offered him a partnership, but Oswald, believing that he had been called by God to mission work, declined.

Instead, he applied to study at the Bible Training Institute (today the Laidlaw College) in Auckland, with the eventual aim of going to South America as a missionary. Six months into his study, however, he had to drop out and return home when his father fell ill. His brother had moved abroad and his sister had married, so Oswald needed to work to support his parents. He gained employment with another law firm, this time under a prominent lawyer who was also a lay preacher.

By this time, Oswald had witnessed several instances of God's provision and guidance in his life, but now he began to experience what it really meant to trust God.

In 1925, Joseph Kemp, the founding principal of Bible Training Institute, invited him to join its staff. At first, Oswald turned down the offer, saying that he had to take care of his father. But he promised to pray over the matter, and two weeks later, felt a strong conviction that God wanted him to say yes. Oswald did, and shortly after, his father recovered.

"God thus graciously confirmed my guidance," he wrote later. "But the confirmation came only after I had stepped out in faith."[3] It was a lesson that Oswald would never forget—and one that he would experience again and again in his life. Later, he would challenge others: "If we could see the way through, it would not be a step of faith. Did Hudson Taylor see the way through when he took that first mighty step of faith? His eyes were on the Lord, not on the way stretching at his feet . . . God is calling us to go forward, what is your response?"[4]

At the college, Oswald took on the role of treasurer and secretary, which included supervising the construction of new college buildings, raising funds, and mentoring students. He also began to deliver lectures on theology; since he had no formal qualifications, he had to master the subject on his own. Oswald's success in both the teaching and administrative fields saw him become the college superintendent in 1931. Two years later, when Kemp died, he took over the top post.

While helming the college, Oswald also found opportunities to fulfil his original promise to the Lord—though somewhat indirectly. He continued to evangelise and speak at conventions, supported missionary organisations, and helped to form the United Maori Mission in 1936.

In a speech on Missionary Day in 1939, he noted, "I entered the New Zealand Bible Institute intending to go to South America as a missionary, but the Lord didn't accept the offering of my life for that purpose, and sent me back to business. It was a great disappointment to me at first . . . But I thank God today that although I am not a missionary, yet I can do something to help missionaries."[5]

Oswald was beginning to realise that while God had indeed called him to missions, it would not be as a worker in the field. And when that call came, it would demand everything of him.

Joining the CIM

In 1945, Bishop Frank Houghton, the General Director of the China Inland Mission, issued a challenge that turned Oswald's world upside down: join the CIM as the Home Director for Australia and New Zealand.

By this time, Oswald had long been involved with CIM work, but not as a full-time staff member. His previous employer at the law firm, John Wilkinson, was the chairman of CIM's New Zealand council, and had frequently got Oswald to help out with secretarial and administrative work. After dealing with local missionaries and donors, and arranging meetings and visits, Oswald had joined as a council member. But now, Bishop Houghton was asking him to join the agency full-time.

To be honest, it wasn't the best moment for such a drastic change. Oswald's family had expanded—he had married Edith Dobson in 1931 and they now had a nine-year-old son, John Wilbur—and they would have to uproot and move to Australia.

Besides, he was doing well at the Bible Training Institute, and the thought of leaving was unthinkable. Friends and relatives also discouraged him from moving. "Why, you would be leaving a larger job for a smaller," they opined.[6] Others suggested that God would hardly enrich the CIM by depriving the college of a good principal and leader.

But as Oswald and Edith prayed over the offer, they felt that this was what God wanted for them. So, despite all the logical arguments against it, Oswald decided to accept the offer. It was only then—after he had stepped out in faith—that the Lord began to smooth his path and confirm that he had made the right choice. Worries about who would take over the college were eased when a suitable successor was found, and a debt that the college owed for the construction of a new building was miraculously paid for by a donor just before he left. Then, when the Sanders moved to Melbourne in Australia, God provided a nice home even though housing was difficult to obtain at the time. Friends and relatives, meanwhile, started to change their minds and now affirmed his decision.

"We had to take the initial step of faith without any tangible confirmations and against the original opinion of our friends, and this was not easy," Oswald wrote later. "But subsequent events provided us with absolute assurance that we had moved in the will of God."[7]

But this was just the beginning of the journey. While Oswald had experience working in law firms and heading a Bible college, he found that dealing with missionaries was different. He had no field experience, and his well-ordered and business-like approach to problem-solving was not always popular, especially among some of the older missionaries. Over time, however, most of them began to value his decisiveness, insightful mind, and ability to get to the heart of any issue at hand. What made him stand out even more was his preaching and speaking; his sermons and speeches continued to touch, inspire, and galvanise those who heard them.

Then the May 1954 letter arrived, inviting Oswald to take the top post in the CIM. Remembering how God had repeatedly empowered him to take on seemingly impossible challenges in the past, he restrained himself from turning it down on the spot and, together with Edith, put it to much prayer. This time, God gave him several prods to show him that no matter what doubts he, Oswald, had about the job, God would see him through yet again.

Just as Edith was telling him that the move appeared to be "inevitable", an old friend who had been staying with Oswald quoted from 1 Peter 5:1–7, where Peter exhorts elders to shepherd the flock with the right attitude. Oswald was particularly struck by how the passage read in the J. B. Phillips version of the Bible: "Accept the responsibility of looking after them willingly and not because you feel you can't get out of it . . . You can throw the whole weight of your anxieties upon him, for you are his personal concern".[8]

The words came like a blow. Clearly, God was telling him to accept the responsibility with the right heart, while at the same time giving him assurance that He would walk with him throughout the journey.

It was an assurance that Oswald would find himself drawing on deeply over the next 15 years, as he led the missions agency through the challenges it was facing on many different fronts. China was, for the time being, off-limits to its missionaries, and the CIM was pondering its future and considering ministering in Japan, Taiwan, Indonesia, Philippines, Thailand, and Malaysia. Internally, the organisation was grappling with a major restructuring of its leadership roles and responsibilities. Oswald had to travel around the region extensively, visiting missionaries to gain an understanding of their work, challenges, and needs—and to convince them of the need to adapt to the changing world. He also had to work with the various councils overseeing the different countries and regions—each with its own unique culture, traditions, and set of challenges—all the while attempting to keep the entire agency united.

Throughout his leadership of the CIM, Oswald would repeatedly feel overwhelmed by a sense of inadequacy. But, as he discovered, this fear of not being up to the job could be an asset: it was a constant reminder to look to the Lord for help and to rely on Him completely.

"It all depends on your attitude to it," he once wrote. "I've found that when the Lord has asked me to do some new thing for which I've not had the qualifications; when in conscious inadequacy I've turned to the Lord and said, 'Well, Lord, You're calling me to do it and I'm looking to You to provide,' then, in every case He's seen me through. That's one of the lessons of inadequacy. It's not something that the Lord takes away. He doesn't necessarily make you feel adequate, but He does see you through."[9]

Oswald's Legacy

Oswald's accomplishments were very different from those of missionaries in the field. While Oswald had dedicated himself to missionary service, God's calling for him was not to go out into the field as a harvester, but to be a sender, a leader, an encourager, and an enabler.

God gave Oswald formidable leadership, administrative, and diplomacy skills—and the opportunity to make full use of them. Over his 15 years as General Director, Oswald led the CIM through one of its most difficult times, helping to reshape, re-organise, and nurture it into a truly international missions agency. His efficiency, powers of reason and planning, and willingness to listen to people helped the missions agency evolve in tandem with a growing church, especially in Asia. Indeed, one of Oswald's legacies was bringing Asian missionaries into the fold. Up till then, the agency had been primarily a Western body serving in an Eastern field. Oswald saw that the CIM needed to welcome, encourage, and send out a new generation of Asian believers who were raring to spread the gospel in the region—a revolutionary concept at the time.

Reflecting the growth and expansion of its harvest field, the CIM was renamed the Overseas Missionary Fellowship in 1964 and OMF International in 1993. Today, the OMF continues to send out and support more than a thousand missionaries from over 30 nations.

Oswald's involvement in missions did not stop when he stepped down from the OMF in 1969. At the age of 70, he became the principal of the Christian Leaders' Training College in Papua New Guinea, nurturing it so that it could be turned over to local leadership when Papua New Guinea gained its independence three years later.

Ironically, it was arguably as a writer that Oswald is most remembered. Dabbling in the written ministry as early as 1925, when he helped a friend start a small Christian monthly periodical, whet his appetite for writing. A powerful speaker, he had much content and many insights to put to paper. His first book, *The Divine Art of Soul-Winning*, a compilation of his lectures, was published in 1937. It did so well that many requests came in for a second book, which came out the following year. All in all, he would write more than 30 books—an amazing feat, considering the responsibilities and workload he was shouldering at the Bible Institute and CIM. More than two million copies of Oswald's books have been printed, and they have been translated into more than 20 languages.

In their biography of Oswald, *To Fight Better*, writers Ron and Gwen Roberts note that the most important lesson to learn from Oswald's life is not what great things a man can do for God; rather, it is about how God can work through a man who repeatedly felt inadequate for the tasks he was called to do.

Throughout his life, Oswald had come to God many times to say that he couldn't take the pressure. God had not always removed such pressures, but He had always given Oswald the faith and strength to live by His grace.

The story of John Oswald Sanders, the biography notes, is "essentially a story of divine sovereignty at work in the life of one man, shaping and preparing him for service. It is the story of a man who . . . placed himself and all his concerns under God's control. It is not only the story of what God could do with a man of exceptional gifts and above average energy and drive. Rather it is the story of what God can do with any life, at any level, no matter how ordinary it may seem, that is prepared to allow God to take the controls through all the checkered ways of life."[10]

A Hard Decision
Eugene Wee

At the age of 26, Eugene Wee left a well-paying job in Singapore to start Radion International, a Christian non-profit organisation involved in rehabilitation, community education, and humanitarian assistance. He tells the story of how God called him.

At the age of 16, I sat in church listening to a preacher talking about reaching drug addicts, prostitutes, and street children—people who are often shunned in society and even by the church. When I heard this, tears flowed from my eyes. I realised that there were people out there who really needed hope and Christ.

As I sat there, I made a vow to the Lord, "If you call, I'll follow, no matter what the cost or how painful." Since then, the thought of going into full-time ministry had always been on my mind, a lingering thought that refused to go away.

Between the vow and the call, there was a 10-year gap. Like most people, I pursued all the finer things in life, hoping that material things would bring purpose and meaning to my life. But the opposite happened. As my life got more cluttered with the things of the world, the sense of emptiness became stronger. I was doing well in my career, but there was a deep emptiness inside. I often wondered if a nice career, car, and wine was all there was to life and what they would all mean at the end of the day. What would I say when I stood in front of my Maker? That I had invested my entire life chasing after the glitter of the world?

It took a series of events, rather than a single encounter, to stir me to go into missions.

The first came when I was trekking up a volcano in Indonesia. While I was well equipped, the local guide wore an oversized jacket and torn shoes that barely fit his small feet. As we walked, he would stop ever so often to show me the flowers and animals, and exclaim, "Isn't it beautiful, Mr Wee?"

I couldn't see it. To me, it was just a common forest. All I wanted was to go to the top.

But the guide seemed to love every minute of the walk. It piqued my curiosity, and I had to ask him: "You speak excellent English, and working as a mountain guide probably does not earn you as much as you could in the bigger towns. Why do you do it?"

He smiled and replied, "Yes, my wife tells me that too! This job doesn't pay much, but it puts food on the table and puts my kids through school. I can live simply, and what better job is there that allows you to walk in places you love and to show them to people like yourself?"

After that conversation, I started to pay more attention to my surroundings. I realised that if all we are seeing is the top of the mountain, we may miss some of the most beautiful parts of life. Often, we are so busy running after goals that seem to matter— like our stock portfolios, what cars we drive, what houses we live in, our annual incomes—that at the end of our journey, we find that we have not really lived, never mind impacted someone else's life.

The second turning point came after a volunteer stint helping the Hmong people in Thailand. When I spent time researching their history, my heart bled. There were just so many needs and so many social issues, yet they received so little help. They represented people close to God's heart—those who have been stigmatised, misunderstood, and unreached. Christ died for them as well.

It reminded me of the vow I had made when I was 16. So often, we tell God that we would follow Him to the ends of the world, but do we really mean it? I was torn between my career and going up to the mountains to do something.

The third turning point came one Sunday after the trip to Thailand. At church, the preacher spoke from the book of Haggai and read 1:8: "Go up into the mountains . . . and build". My heart broke. I felt the Lord was calling me to make haste and go. But there was so much at stake, and I wanted to be sure. So, before the service ended, I asked the Lord for a clear confirmation. "If You say it again, 'Go up to the mountains and build', I will go," I prayed. As it was unusual to hear a sermon on Haggai, a very short book, I knew it would be close to impossible to hear it preached over two consecutive weeks.

The following week, when the same preacher walked up to the pulpit, my heart skipped a beat. The chances of hearing Haggai 1:8 again were low, I told myself. Then she opened the Bible to the book of Haggai. My heart started racing. There was still a chance God would not call me. Teaching series normally go forward and not back to the same verses. But then I heard the words, "Go up into the mountains . . . and build". I knew I had to answer the call.

It was an extremely hard decision to make. In fact, "hard" was an understatement. There is so much to hold on to in Singapore. Putting it all aside is contrary to everything we have been brought up to pursue. I used to joke with my Christian friends that when I first heard the call, tears rolled down my cheeks—tears of pain.

Before tendering my resignation, I walked over to a colleague who was a fellow believer. Without saying much, I just asked him, "Would God even use a wretched person like me?" Without looking up, he calmly replied, "If God thinks you are qualified, you are. That is all that matters."

We often have a romanticised idea of missions. We yearn for the greatest harvest, but shun the hard work of sowing.

Going into missions has cost me dearly. I have been in despair, pain, and tears. I have suffered broken relationships. I have been discouraged and misunderstood. I've been labelled as a rebel, told that I didn't have a "missions track record", and advised to "get a proper job and don't waste your life away". But I've lost the deep craving for the glitter of the world that so easily entwines a man.

Yes, it's been painful. But if I had a chance to turn back time, I would gladly do it all over again.

Sources

One

A Significant Death Adoniram Judson

Bibliography

1. "Adoniram Judson, First Missionary from the United States". *Christianity*. Last accessed 6 July 2017. http://www.christianity.com/church/church-history/church-history-for-kids/adoniram-judson-first-missionary-from-the-united-states-11635044.html.

2. "Adoniram Judson". *Wikipedia*. Edited 23 June 2017. https://en.wikipedia.org/wiki/Adoniram_Judson.

3. Barlow, Fred. "Adoniram Judson: Father of Baptist Missions". In *Profiles in Evangelism*. Murfreesboro, TN: Sword of the Lord Publishers, 1976. http://www.wholesomewords.org/missions/bjudson1.html.

4. Federer, Bill. "Death of a Friend Led to Surprising Birth". *World Net Daily*. Posted 18 February, 2017. http://www.wnd.com/2017/02/death-of-a-friend-led-to-surprising-birth/.

5. Harrison, Eugene Myers. "Adoniram Judson (1788–1850): Apostle of the Love of Christ in Burma". *Reformed Reader*. Edited 10 August 2014. http://www.reformedreader.org/rbb/judson/ajbio.htm.

6. Pierard, Richard. "The Man Who Gave the Bible to the Burmese". *Christianity Today*, no. 90 (2006). http://www.christianitytoday.com/history/issues/issue-90/man-who-gave-bible-to-burmese.html.

7. Piper, John. "How Few There Are Who Die So Hard!". *Desiring God*. Posted 4 February 2003. http://www.desiringgod.org/messages/how-few-there-are-who-die-so-hard.

Endnotes

[1] Piper, "How Few There Are Who Die So Hard!".

[2] Harrison, "Adoniram Judson".

[3] Ibid.

[4] Ibid.

[5] Ibid.

[6] Ibid.

Two

Going Native George Leslie Mackay

Bibliography

1. "Aletheia University". *Wikipedia*. Edited 30 June 2017. https://en.wikipedia.org/wiki/Aletheia_University.

2. "George Leslie Mackay". *Wikipedia*. Edited 21 June 2017. https://en.wikipedia.org/wiki/George_Leslie_Mackay.

3. Austin, Alvyn J. "Mackay, George Leslie". In *Dictionary of Canadian Biography*. Accessed 6 July 2017. http://www.biographi.ca/en/bio/mackay_george_leslie_13E.html.

4. Forsberg, Clyde R. Jr., ed. *The Life and Legacy of George Leslie Mackay: An Interdisciplinary Study of Canada's First Presbyterian Missionary to Northern Taiwan (1872–1901)*. Newcastle: Cambridge Scholars Publishing, 2012. http://www.cambridgescholars.com/the-life-and-legacy-of-george-leslie-mackay-14.

5. Kellenberger, Carrie. "The Legacy of George Leslie Mackay". Canadian Chamber of Commerce in Taiwan. Posted 27 February 2016. https://www.canchamtw.com/the-legacy-of-george-leslie-mackay/.

6. Mackay, George Leslie. *From Far Formosa: The Island, Its People, and Missions*. Edited by J. A. Macdonald. Toronto: Fleming H. Revell, 1896.

7. PEKHO. "Rev. Dr George Leslie Mackay". *The Taiwanese* (blog). Posted 20 March 2006. http://thetaiwanese.blogspot.sg/2006/03/rev-dr-george-leslie-mackay.html.

8.   Rohrer, James R. "The Legacy of George Leslie Mackay". *International Bulletin of Missionary Research* 34, no. 4 (2010): 221–228. http://www.internationalbulletin. org/issues/2010-04/2010-04-221-rohrer.html.

Endnotes

[1] Mackay, From Far Formosa, 92.

[2] Austin, "Mackay, George Leslie".

[3] Mackay, *From Far Formosa*, 142.

[4] Ibid., 16.

[5] Austin, "Mackay, George Leslie".

[6] Mackay, *From Far Formosa*, 285.

[7] Austin, "Mackay, George Leslie".

[8] Annie Straith Jamieson, *Some Things That Should Be Known to the Ladies of the Women's Foreign Missionary Society in Canada* (Hong Kong, 1888), 9. Quoted in Rohrer, "The Legacy of George Leslie Mackay".

[9] Mackay, *From Far Formosa*, 324–325.

[10] Rohrer, "The Legacy of George Leslie Mackay".

[11] Mackay, *From Far Formosa*, 13.

[12] Kellenberger, "The Legacy of George Leslie Mackay".

Three

The Call of the Wild: James Matthew Hoover

Bibliography

1.   David W. Scott. *Mission as Globalization: Methodists in Southeast Asia at the Turn of the Twentieth Century*. New York: Lexington Books, 2016.

2.   Ernest Lau. *From Mission to Church: The Evolution of the Methodist Church in Singapore and Malaysia: 1885–1976*. Singapore: Genesis Books, 2008.

3.   Frank T. Cartwright. *Tuan Hoover of Borneo*. New York: The Abingdon Press, 1938.

4.   Gerald H. Anderson, ed. *Biographical Dictionary of Christian Missions*. Michigan: William B. Eerdmans Publishing Company, 1999.

5. C. Micheal Hawn, "Through Every Land: Missionaries—It's Complicated". *Mhawnblog* (blog). Posted 13 May 2016. https://mhawnblog.wordpress. com/2016/05/13/through-every-land-missionaries-its-complicated/.

Endnotes

[1] Cartwright, *Tuan Hoover of Borneo*, 6.

[2] Ibid., 6.

[3] Ibid., 6.

[4] Ibid., 6.

[5] Ibid., 7.

[6] Ibid., 8.

[7] Ibid., 13.

[8] Ibid., 34.

[9] Ibid., 36.

[10] Ibid., 61.

Four

Into the Madhouse John Sung

Bibliography

1. "John Sung (1901–1944)". Gospel Fellowship Association Missions. Posted 22 May 1998. http://www.gfamissions.org/pages/learn-and-promote/detail/3/66/.

2. "John Sung". *Wikipedia*. Edited 13 May 2017. https://en.wikipedia.org/wiki/ John_Sung.

3. Doyle, G. Wright. "John Song (Sung Shangjie) (1901–1944)". *Biographical Dictionary of Chinese Christianity*. Edited 1 December 2016. http://www.bdcconline.net/en/ stories/s/song-shangjie.php.

4. Graves, Dan. "Death of Amazing Chinese Evangelist John Sung". *Christianity*. Edited July 2007. http://www.christianity.com/church/church-history/ timeline/1901-2000/death-of-amazing-chinese-evangelist-john-sung-11630778. html.

5. Hymers, R. L., Jr. "The Real Conversion of Dr John Sung". Sermon, Baptist Tabernacle of Los Angeles, 6 June 2009. http://www.rlhymersjr.com/Online_Sermons/2009/060609PM_JohnSung.html.

6. Lim Ka-Tong. *The Life and Ministry of John Sung*. Singapore: Armour Publishing, 2011.

7. Lyall, Leslie T. *A Biography of John Sung*. Singapore: Armour Publishing, 2004.

8. Song Shangjie. *The Diary of John Sung: Extracts from His Journals and Notes*. Singapore: Armour Publishing, 2012.

9. Tow, Timothy. Translator's preface to "Forty John Sung Revival Sermons". Home of Grace. Accessed 7 July 2017. http://www.hograce.org/eng/document/Song.Sermons/v1/preface.htm.

10. Tow, Timothy. *John Sung My Teacher*. Singapore: Christian Life Publishers, 1985. http://www.truelifebpc.org.sg/he_being_dead_yet_speaketh/Contents/4%20-%20Books%20&%20Publications/John%20Sung%20My%20Teacher.pdf.

11. Tow, Timothy. "John Sung and the Asian Awakening". *Revivals in ACS(I) Singapore* (blog). Posted 1 July 2001. https://acsirevivals.wordpress.com/other-revivals/the-asian-awakening-john-sung-revival/.

End Notes

[1] Lyall, *A Biography of John Sung*, 35.

[2] Hymers, "The Real Conversion of Dr John Sung".

[3] Ibid.

[4] Lyall, *A Biography of John Sung*, 43.

[5] Tow, translator's preface to "Forty John Sung Revival Sermons".

[6] Doyle, "John Song".

[7] Hymers, "The Real Conversion of Dr John Sung".

[8] Graves, "Death of Amazing Chinese Evangelist John Sung".

[9] Hymers, "The Real Conversion of Dr John Sung".

[10] William E. Schubert, *I Remember John Sung* (Singapore: Far Eastern Bible College Press, 1976), 14. Quoted in Lyall, *A Biography of John Sung*, xi.

Five

The "Failed" Missionary Gladys May Aylward

Bibliography

1. "Gladys Aylward". Pacific Baptist Church. Accessed 7 July 2017. http://www. pacificbaptist.com/missions/gladys-aylward.pdf.

2. "Gladys Aylward". *Wikipedia*. Accessed 6 July 2017. https://en.wikipedia.org/wiki/ Gladys_Aylward.

3. "Gladys Aylward's Long Road to China". *Christianity*. Accessed 6 July 2017. http:// www.christianity.com/church/church-history/church-history-for-kids/gladys-aylwards-long-road-to-china-11634863.html.

4. "Missionary Quotes". Youth with a Mission Salem. Accessed 7 July 2017. http:// www.ywamsalem.org/wp-content/uploads/2015/05/Missionary-Quotes.pdf.

5. Aylward, Gladys. *Gladys Aylward: The Little Woman*. Chicago: Moody Press, 1970. http://bibleteachingprogram.com/btp/life/gifts/giftsweb/aylward1.htm.

6. Baines, Francesca. "Aylward, Gladys (1902–1970)". *Encyclopedia*. Accessed 7 July 2017. http://www.encyclopedia.com/women/encyclopedias-almanacs-transcripts-and-maps/aylward-gladys-1902-1970.

7. Benge, Janet, and Geoff. *Gladys Aylward: The Adventure of a Lifetime*. Seattle: YWAM Publications, 1998.

8. Burgess, Alan. *The Small Woman*. London: Evans Brothers, 1957.

9. Covell, Ralph R. "Gladys May Aylward (Ai Weide) 1902–1970". *Biographical Dictionary of Chinese Christianity*. Accessed 6 July 2017. http://www.bdcconline.net/ en/stories/a/aylward-gladys.php.

10. Fritzius, John M. "Gladys Aylward (1902–1970)". *Tlogical*. Accessed 7 July 2017. http://www.tlogical.net/bioaylward.htm.

11. Grant, Myrna. *Gladys Aylward: No Mountain Too High*. Fearn, UK: Christian Focus Publications, 2003.

12. Kiefer, James E. "Gladys Aylward, Missionary to China (3 January 1970)". *Biographical Sketches of Memorable Christians of the Past*. Accessed 6 July 2017. http:// justus.anglican.org/resources/bio/73.html.

13. Latham, Robert O. *Gladys Aylward, One of the Undefeated: The Story of Gladys Aylward as Told by Her to R. O. Latham*. London: Edinburgh House Press, 1950.

14. Purves, Carol. *Chinese Whispers: The Gladys Aylward Story.* Herefordshire, UK: Day One Publications, 2004. http://dougnichols.org/wp/wp-content/uploads/2013/12/Chinese-Whispers-G-Aylward-Story-1.pdf.

15. Swift, Catherine. *Gladys Aylward: The Courageous English Missionary Whose Life Defied All Expectations.* Bloomington, MN: Bethany House Publishers, 1989.

16. Voelkel, Jack. "Gladys Aylward: Small Woman, Big Heart, Great Faith". *Urbana* (blog). Posted 18 November 2007. https://urbana.org/blog/gladys-aylward.

17. Wellman, Sam. *Gladys Aylward: Missionary to China.* Uhrichsville, OH: Barbour Publishing, 1998.

End Notes

[1] Burgess, *The Small Woman*, 15–16.

[2] Ibid., 16.

[3] Ibid., 17.

[4] Aylward, *Gladys Aylward*, 7–8.

[5] Ibid., 8.

[6] Ibid., 8.

[7] Burgess, *The Small Woman*, 16–17.

[8] Aylward, *Gladys Aylward*, 9.

[9] Ibid., 9.

[10] Ibid., 11–12.

[11] Ibid., 12.

[12] Burgess, *The Small Woman*, 21.

[13] Purves, *Chinese Whispers*, 19.

[14] Aylward, *Gladys Aylward*, 15.

[15] Burgess, *The Small Woman*, 25.

[16] Ibid., 80.

[17] Ibid., 89–90.

[18] Baines, "Aylward, Gladys".

[19] Burgess, *The Small Woman*, 144.

[20] Wellman, *Gladys Aylward*, 191.

[21] Aylward, *Gladys Aylward*, 9.

[22] "Missionary Quotes." Youth with a Mission Salem.

Six

The Difficult Visitors Ludwig Ingwer Nommensen

Bibliography

1. "Batak Protestant Christian Church". *Encyclopaedia Britannica*. Accessed 11 August 2017. https://www.britannica.com/topic/Batak-Protestant-Christian-Church#ref148658.

2. "Birth of Heroic Missionary Ludwig Nommensen (1834)". Christian History Institute. Posted 6 February 2017. https://www.christianhistoryinstitute.org/it-happened-today/2/6/.

3. "Ludwig Ingwer Nommensen: An Apostle for the Batak". *Asienreisender*. Posted 26 August 2014. http://www.asienreisender.de/nommensen.html.

4. "Ludwig Ingwer Nommensen". *Wikipedia*. Edited 26 December 2016. https://en.wikipedia.org/wiki/Ludwig_Ingwer_Nommensen.

5. "Nommensen, Ingwer Ludwig (1834–1918): Pioneer Missionary to the Batak in Sumatra". Boston University School of Theology. Accessed 11 August 2017. http://www.bu.edu/missiology/missionary-biography/n-o-p-q/nommensen-ingwer-ludwig-1834-1918/.

6. Halloran, Kevin. "Eaten by Cannibals—Used Mightily by God". *Anchored in Christ* (Blog). Posted 15 October 2014. http://www.kevinhalloran.net/the-story-of-ludwig-nommensen/.

7. Kiefer, James E. "Ludwig Nommensen, Missionary to Sumatra". Society of Archbishop Justus. Accessed 11 August 2017. http://justus.anglican.org/resources/bio/163.html.

8. Lehmann, Martin E. "Focus on the Family". *In A Biographical Study of Ingwer Ludwig Nommensen 1834–1918: Pioneer Missionary to the Bataks of Sumatra*. Lewiston, New York: Edwin Mellen Press, 1996.

9. Nommensen, Timothy L. "Ludwig Ingwer Nommensen and the Batak Church in Sumatra". Essay, Wisconsin Lutheran Seminary, 1987. http://www.wlsessays.net/bitstream/handle/123456789/3492/NommensenLINommensenBatakSumatra.pdf?sequence=1&isAllowed=y.

10. Schreiner, Lothar. "Nommensen, Ingwer Ludwig". *In Biographical Dictionary of Christian Missions. Edited by Gerald H. Anderson.* New York: Macmillan Reference USA, 1998.

11. Schreiner, Lothar. "The Legacy of Ingwer Ludwig Nommensen". *International Bulletin of Missionary Research*, February 2000. http://www.internationalbulletin. org/issues/2000-02/2000-02-081-schreiner.pdf.

End Notes

[1] Nommensen, "Ludwig Ingwer Nommensen and the Batak Church in Sumatra", 20.

[2] Ibid., 12.

[3] Schreiner, "The Legacy of Ingwer Ludwig Nommensen".

[4] Nommensen, "Ludwig Ingwer Nommensen and the Batak Church in Sumatra", 2.

[5] Ibid., 3.

[6] Ibid., 4.

[7] Ibid., 7.

[8] Ibid., 14.

[9] Ibid., 28.

[10] Ibid., 28.

Seven

An Indefinite Plan Sophia Blackmore

Bibliography

1. "Sophia Blackmore". *Roots.* Accessed 11 August 2017. https://roots.sg/learn/ resources/publications/singapore-council-of-womens-organisations/01-sophia-blackmore.

2. "Sophia Blackmore". *Wikipedia.* Edited 11 March 2017. https://en.wikipedia.org/ wiki/Sophia_Blackmore.

3. Doraisamy, Theodore R., ed. *Sophia Blackmore in Singapore: Educational and Missionary Pioneer 1887–1927.* Singapore: General Conference Women's Society of Christian Service, Methodist Church of Singapore, 1987.

4. Frost, Mark Ravinder and Yu-Mei Balasingamchow. *Singapore: A Biography*. Singapore: Didier Millet & Hong Kong University Press, 2009.

5. Lau, Earnest. *From Mission to Church: The Evolution of the Methodist Church in Singapore*. Malaysia: Armour Publishing, 2008.

6. Lau, Ernest. *Sophia Blackmore*. Singapore: Methodist Church of Singapore, 1995. http://www.trac-mcs.org.sg/images/pdf/boardofministry/Sophia%20Blackmore.pdf.

7. Tan, Bonny. "Sophia Blackmore". National Library Board. Posted 2008. http://eresources.nlb.gov.sg/infopedia/articles/SIP_1339_2008-10-10.html.

8. Tym, "Book preview: The education of Singapore girls". *Singapore: A Biography* (blog). Posted 5 October 2009. http://www.singaporebiography.com/labels/Modern%20Times.html.

End Notes

[1] Doraisamy, *Sophia Blackmore in Singapore*, 4.

[2] Ibid., 2.

[3] Ibid., 3.

[4] Ibid.,63.

[5] Ibid., 5.

[6] Ibid., 63.

[7] Ibid., 16.

[8] Ibid., 22.

[9] Ibid., 61.

[10] Ibid., 66.

[11] Ibid., iii.

Eight

The Inadequate Leader Oswald Sanders

Bibliography

1. "John Oswald Sanders". *Wikipedia*. Edited 23 January 2017. https://en.wikipedia.org/wiki/John_Oswald_Sanders.

2. Lineham, Peter J. "Sanders, John Oswald". *Te Ara: The Encyclopedia of New Zealand*. Accessed 28 August 2017. https://teara.govt.nz/en/biographies/4s3/sanders-john-oswald.

3. Roberts, Ron and Gwen Roberts. *To Fight Better*. Great Britain: Highland Books/ Overseas Missionary Fellowship, 1989.

4. Sanders, J. Oswald. *This I Remember*. Eastbourne, Great Britain: Kingsway Publications, 1982.

End Notes

[1] Sanders, J. Oswald. *This I Remember*, 20.

[2] Roberts and Roberts, *To Fight Better*, 29.

[3] Sanders, J. Oswald. *This I Remember*, 17.

[4] Roberts and Roberts, *To Fight Better*, 133.

[5] Ibid., 84.

[6] Ibid., 82.

[7] Sanders, J. Oswald. *This I Remember*, 19.

[8] Roberts and Roberts, *To Fight Better*, 105.

[9] Ibid., 61.

[10] Ibid., 190.

ABOUT THE PUBLISHER

Discovery House Publishing™ produces a wide array of
premium and quality resources that focus on Scripture,
show reverence for God and His Word, demonstrate the relevance
of vibrant faith, and equip and encourage you to draw closer
to God in all seasons of your life.

NOTE TO THE READER

We invite you to share your response to the message in this book
by writing to us at:
5 Pereira Road, #07-01
Asiawide Industrial Building
Singapore 368025

or send e-mail to
dhpsingapore@dhp.org